PURPOSE THROUGH PAIN

FINDING LIMITLESS POTENTIAL
IN THE PRESENCE OF ADVERSITY

JUSTEN ARNOLD

TWO PENNY
PUBLISHING

Two Penny
PUBLISHING

An imprint of Two Penny Publishing
twopennypublishing.com

For information about the author, book events, or interviews,
please contact the author representative at:
info@twopennypublishing.com

Scripture quotations marked NLT are taken from the Holy Bible,
New Living Translation. © 1996, 2004, 2007, 2013, 2015 by Tyndale
House Foundation. Used by permission of Tyndale House Publishers,
Inc., Carol Stream, Illinois 60188. All rights reserved.

Scripture quotations marked NIV are taken from the Holy Bible,
New International Version®, NIV®. Copyright © 1973, 1978, 1984,
2011 by Biblica, Inc.™ Used by permission of Zondervan. All rights
reserved worldwide. www.zondervan.com. The "NIV" and
"New International Version" are trademarks registered in the
United States Patent and Trademark Office by Biblica, Inc.™

Library of Congress Control Number: 2021920740

ISBN: 978-1-950995-53-0
Also available in Ebook

Printed in the United States of America
FIRST EDITION

table of contents

This book would never have come to fruition and,
therefore, not be in your hands right now if not for my wife
Alexis, kids, and good friend Justin Hemming!

You were my motivation and support even when starting to put
pen to paper. YES, ALL OF YOU (even you Ayva). You all had
more confidence in me than I sometimes had in myself. Without
your spark, love, guidance, and patience, I could not have written
one page of this book. So for that, I dedicate this book to you.

endorsements

From the moment I met Justen, I was captured by his amazing energy and spirit. He has an infinite ability to care for others while honoring all his responsibilities in life. He is a wonderful, faithful man! Be ready to be inspired, uplifted, and enlightened by Justen's story as you turn each page.

Karen Lathigee Blank

B.S., Public Health, ACE CPT

Justen is one of the most genuine, passionate people I know. In my humble opinion, he's a shining example of how you can be a great family man, a great businessman, and have a fulfilling life all at the same time! His quest to change people's lives for the better, and do it with integrity, is refreshing in this day and age.

Marc Zalmanoff

Coach, Author, Entrepreneur

Justen Arnold is a man who cares about others and wants only their best. He's endured, and now he shares. We are all sure to be blessed.

Chuck Sackett

Professor, Lincoln Christian University Preaching Team,
Madison Park Christian Church Adjunct Faculty, TCMI Intl.

In today's modern world, it's rare to find a man of high integrity. A true Renaissance man. A father, a husband, an entrepreneur, and a true friend. Justen is a man who approaches all of these roles with grace and creativity.

When Justen first told me he was writing a book, I couldn't wait to hear his story as I knew it would uplift humanity. This is a mission we both share, and I'm honored and thrilled to endorse Justen Arnold.

Carolyn Hori

Intuitive Coach and Founder of *Give Your Soulless Job the Pink Slip*

Justen Arnold and I participate in a weekly Men's Group (The Master Mind Group). The purpose of the group is to become better men and people. Over several years I have learned a lot about Justen. He is ambitious, consistent, honest, courageous, humble, has a positive mindset, leads by example, is of service to others, puts his family first, and has unshakable faith. Since joining the group, Justen has helped me in my journey more than he knows.

Mike LaRocca

Attorney Agent/Principal with Ryker Joseph & Brick

I appreciate Justen's desire and drive to, by God's grace, push through pain and difficulty, learn, grow, and help others do the same. He's a crazy hard worker who loves to help others."

Andy Woodall

Pastor of Marriage and Counseling

Justen is the epitome of a leader. He is willing to be open, vulnerable, and authentic in order to serve others and bring healing to a world in pain. His story and teachings will help people in ways that will ripple across
the world.

Brian Costello
Founder and CEO of O23 Holistic Systems

Justen is truly one of those people that will give you the shirt off his back if you need it. He looks for the best in every person. He is one of the first, if not the first person I ask for advice from when I need advice and encouragement. I feel lucky to be able to call him a close friend. I am excited to learn as much as I can from him.

Jonathan L.
Police Officer

foreword

I've had the privilege of knowing Justen for 20 plus years. When on e's friendship extends into decades, you know you have something special. We've seen one another through many ups and downs in life. We've celebrated and mourned many times together.

Justen accompanied me to the Dominican Republic to teach business classes to budding entrepreneurs a few years back. After not seeing one another, we had a blast being in person, which happens when friends move away from their hometowns. The entrepreneurs all loved him and gained a lot from his experience and teaching from first-hand knowledge. It made his teaching feel real rather than just theory, weaving in his first-hand experience alongside the curriculum.

What caught me off guard was Justen's levels of positivity and energy. As I said, we hadn't seen each other in quite some time, and I had forgotten just how positive and energetic he was. Again, the entrepreneurs loved him for that positive energy and were really blessed by it. He even led them in some stretches before our afternoon sessions to get the blood flowing after lunch. We all really enjoyed doing some movement in the middle of the day, albeit with a few of us struggling more than others. I jokingly called him the Energizer Bunny™. He lives what he writes in this book, and I can attest to this first-hand.

Justen shared a bit of his upbringing with me on the plane ride home. Even though we were close, we'd never discussed this part of his life before. Immediately, I knew he could help others by sharing his story. So I encouraged him to write a book.

As he mentions in the following pages, Justen finds inspiration from helping others. I'm beyond excited for him as he releases this book into the world at large. Reading his book has given me a brand new perspective on life. But my biggest takeaway is a sense of hope. I'm sure it will do the same for you.

This book is part memoir, part manual on how to live well. May it give you a real sense of hope and the inspiration to find your own purpose through your pain. As Justen mentions throughout this book, it's not a matter of comparing scars but learning from one another on the road to healing.

Life is loaded with pain and suffering. My prayer is that you will find the best way to move forward in your life through Justen's story and insight.

Justen is a personal trainer but more of a coach, in my opinion. This comes shining through the following pages. I hope you're able to learn from him as he guides us on how to journey through our pain and come out stronger on the other side with a greater sense of purpose.

Justin Hemming

introduction

Welcome to *Purpose Through Pain*, a book about finding limitless potential in the presence of adversity. Thank you for taking the time to pick up or download this book! It is an honor and a blessing for me to share my story and life experience with you. As a gym owner and trainer, I have dedicated my professional life to teaching and challenging others to unleash the power and potential inside themselves. Each day, I bring my training, experience, and education to the gym and hold nothing back from my community. I don't hold anything back because I believe in the boundless potential of each person I encounter. Pouring out everything I have, giving my all, is my approach to training, living, and writing this book.

Stick with me through these chapters, and together we will laugh and cry, contemplate and evaluate, dream and reimagine life with greater success and purpose. I wish we could talk through this together. I would love nothing more than to share stories, listen, and learn from each other. If you are ever in my area, you can find me hiking and adventuring outside with my family or training at my gym, where I still personally lead classes and one-on-one training sessions. I love each opportunity to connect, explore, and grow with other people. I enjoy working with other people, and I help keep them accountable for the growth and goals they set. Our ambition is to move better, feel better, live better. So even though we are not in the gym or on the trail, you can take the stories, experiences, and insights of this book to help you move better, feel better, and live better with endless possibilities.

STORIES OF PAIN & PURPOSE

Through this book, you are going to uncover a story of devastating abuse and physical pain. These stories are tragically real, and I have decided to share them because I believe with all of my heart they will help you, or they can help someone you know. Now more than ever, I am confident that our trauma and pain doesn't define us; it does not limit us. We are not just a collection of things that happen to us. We are so much more than that. The stories I share will show you that potential is limitless in each of us, no matter how broken we feel.

Inside this book, you will uncover a story of life-changing hope and abundant success. *Purpose Through Pain* is more than a title, it is hope, and it is a truth for each of us to live by. As dark as the path gets, we are going to find a light at the end of the tunnel; because unfathomable possibilities are all around you. You are going to get access to insights from my education and training as a gym owner and trainer. You are going to get open and honest accounts from me as a spouse, parent, entrepreneur, and man of faith. I hope you can relate to the best of my experiences and find even higher levels of joy and success than I have.

If you find you can relate to pain, then I want you to know there is hope and purpose for you. No two stories are the same, and there is no point or invitation to compare scars. Each of us has dealt with pain in some way, and it doesn't matter if it looks different. Each of us has immeasurable potential, even if the past insists we don't. My story is one example, and it is the story I know best, so I will share it. After reading through this book, you may feel more inclined to open up about your stories. I hope you find a safe and healthy place to share your experiences. My greatest hope is that something in this book leads you to believe more about yourself and achieve more in the areas of life that matter most.

THE FOUR QUADRANTS OF SUCCESS

In many situations, the term "success" has become too one-dimensional and misunderstood. Typically, we find this focus and attention placed on either fame or fortune. In this book, we will explore and discover a deeper understanding for identifying and defining success, a deeper well for filling your cup. It starts with a multifaceted approach to success, specifically in four key areas. We will call these the four quadrants of success. Each quadrant is a battlefield, an arena full of unique opportunities and obstacles. I'm going to share a brief overview of each quadrant below so you can have an idea of what to expect.

First, we have a *Limitless Family*. As we find limitless potential in ourselves, we will find opportunities to grow and nurture a limitless family. As a husband and a father, I have found life-changing joy and hope through my family. Limitless family is not about the size of your house, the vacations you take, or the number of kids you have. This chapter will show us that we have everything we need. We have all of the time and all of the resources to be great partners and parents. This chapter will focus on the obstacles and limits placed on our family and we will focus on living beyond the limits. We will discover ways to unleash greater potential and success at home. A successful family is all about making the most out of what you have and who you have. No matter what home looked like in your past, your future home and family holds incomprehensible capacity to be limitless.

The second quadrant of success is called *Limitless Finances*. We have to take an honest look at our finances and the power they hold over us. Money is likely one of the greatest limit-setters in your life today. Finances often create barriers for us. Price tags are locks on a door we believe we need to pass through in order to find success or happiness; the problem is there will always be another door with a more expensive lock to open. Debt is an extra set of weight, like baggage that keeps us tied down and stuck in place. There is hope for financial freedom and limitless potential with your finances. In this chapter, we will examine the true nature of finances, identify a healthier mindset and definition for success, and leave the shadows of a bankrupt life. Financial success is ultimately determined by what we do with our money, not how much money we have. No matter what your finances look like today, your financial future holds the power to be filled with abundance without limits.

Third, we have *Limitless Fitness*. Life has broken my body several times, but it has not broken my resolve to move better, feel better, and live better. This quadrant is not just about losing weight or building muscle: we are going to look at a holistic framework for fitness. We are going to address and examine limits in health, exercise, and lifestyle. In this chapter, you are going to receive my expertise and experience as a trainer, gym owner, and lifestyle coach. This will help you to outline plans and practices that will help inspire personal growth and greater fitness in your life. No matter what your fitness looks like today, your future holds limitless potential.

The fourth and final quadrant is *Limitless Faith*. This final chapter and quadrant of success will lean in and examine a deeper level of belief in yourself and who you were meant to be. I, myself, have found a seed of faith and belief that has grown and matured over time. You may be in a different place than I am when it comes to faith and that is perfectly fine. I don't need you to start where I am, I just want you to start somewhere and grow. Finding purpose in pain is not always easy. It is not as simple as flipping a switch and basking in the light. It requires a healthy and growing sense of self-worth, courage, and belief in yourself. And at a certain point, I believe it requires a seed of faith in something bigger than yourself, a belief that God has a purpose for you. Even though we live in a world full of trouble and pain, there is still purpose and joy in the middle of it. In this chapter, we will examine the power of the mind, heart, and soul as we look to grow. No matter how deep your faith is today, your future holds unwavering limitless potential.

GROWTH QUESTIONS & KEY TAKEAWAYS

In this book, you will find my very raw and very real story and find the four quadrants of success. You will also find a series of thought-provoking questions placed all throughout these chapters. Asking questions is a key to learning and growing. Questions don't just give us something to think about, they help us turn our thoughts into actions and realities. Allow for room and time to work through questions, and don't rush past any questions you create for yourself. Find a place to write down your thoughts and the questions you are wrestling with the most. I would also encourage you to find another person or a small group of people to ask these questions with. Doing this can open us up to more perspectives and experiences, and it also can create accountability for decisions and actions we intend to make.

GETTING STARTED

Each day, I get to wake up and explore a new sunrise with my wife and kids. We aim to live life to the fullest, to soak it all in, and to fill our plates with adventure. Every day, every season, there is a fresh new opportunity to live and to grow. As we begin this journey together, I want to encourage you and challenge you to start choosing a full life now. Chapter by chapter, we will unpack my story and how I came to find purpose through pain and limitless potential in the face of adversity. You don't have to wait until the last page to start thinking about personal growth or the next steps. Let each page be a reminder that no matter what the past has held for you or for me, we can use today to move closer towards something greater.

My hope and reason for this book are that maybe, just maybe, something in it will click with you. Something will help you to substantially change your life and how you look at life. It may seem small at first, like many things I do, or even minuscule at times—still the compounding effort of positive actions and development will create a domino effect and compound over time to create big consequences. I like to compare it to evolution in regard to how far human life has grown. I mean, look at humans just within the past few years with technology, and we could even look at it as a decline in some form or fashion, and that's another reason for writing this book. It's not some big cataclysmic event. It's the small positive daily actions of personal development serving and loving others.

chapter one

THE DEVIL OUTSIDE DOING PUSHUPS

"STAY ALERT! WATCH OUT FOR YOUR GREAT ENEMY,
THE DEVIL. HE PROWLS AROUND LIKE A ROARING
LION, LOOKING FOR SOMEONE TO DEVOUR."
1 PETER 5:8 (NLT)

You have limitless potential and purpose.

Don't throw that statement to the side or dismiss it. I hope
something in this book, and the journey we will take together
through it, will spark this truth within you. Do you believe that about
yourself? Your life has potential and purpose. There is something
inside each of us: an inherent identity, a God-given gift of existence.
Throughout my day, and especially in the morning, I take a quiet
moment to breathe and remind myself of this. I take six deep
breaths, and I hold this hope of purpose close to my heart and mind.

What could you accomplish today if you believed your moments hold potential and purpose?

Each day, I am going to encounter opportunities for success in the key areas of my life: family, faith, fitness, and finances. These areas each hold a special value and role in life, and later on, in this book, we will dive into their significance. We each wake up with a full day in front of us, and that is why we call today "the present!" Today is a gift waiting to be opened. And we have the ability to inspire and influence the future gifts of tomorrow. Life is an adventure, and we get to travel through it, unlocking joy and success along the way. No matter the destination, there is joy in the journey. Whether today is a gift or a journey, the truth is there is goodness and success before you. There is potential and purpose in you. The question is, what is stopping you from taking hold of it?

WELCOME TO MY LIFE

Life is good! I have a loving and beautiful family. I believe in myself and my God-given purpose. I am physically fit and healthy. I am financially secure and operate a growing business. Each day offers me more potential for joy and fulfillment. Every season provides opportunities for growth and development. If you could follow me around for a day, then you would see firsthand how blessed this season of life has been. How do I know? People I see daily often tell me this. They also tell me I am one of the most optimistic, energetic, and balanced people they have ever met. I honestly don't feel comfortable writing those words, but it is true.

Life happens moment by moment, day by day, and season by season. This has been a very happy, healthy, and successful season for me. This week I am going to spend time leading and operating my business as a gym owner, trainer, and coach. I am going to play with my kids and go on adventures with them. I will have time to spend with my wife and recognize her many accomplishments. And I will cherish moments to do things that bring me joy. All the while thanking God for all He has given me. This season of life has been full of success and my purpose has been clear.

Each season is a new mountain to climb and a new journey to take. I can set goals for myself, for my family, faith, fitness, and finances. In many ways, the seasons of life are like a series of mountains and adventures. As we climb, we discover new opportunities and challenges along the way. Remember, there is joy in the journey! I can see the goals off in the distance, but it is the moments along the journey that bring the true rewards. This season has been drawing to a close, I know it and I can see it. There are new opportunities forming on the horizon. They are hard to make out, but I have a sense of what they could be. However, opportunity is not the only thing waiting for me on the next climb.

My constant optimism and energy would lead many people to believe that most, if not all, seasons of my life have been good and successful. This is a temptation for all of us. We are inclined to judge someone's entire life based on their current circumstances, good or bad. We make assumptions and even accusations about someone else without even knowing the larger portions of their story. Life is full of moments, days, and seasons—and no two are the same. Our daily encounters are just a snapshot of each other's whole life stories. This is why I need to tell my story; it is why you need to tell your story.

This is why I know, for a fact, that tomorrow and the next season of my life hold more than just opportunity. My life, like yours, is full of potential and purpose. My life is also full of obstacles, pain, and an enemy who wants nothing more than to kick my ass. I am optimistic because I have faced life-changing obstacles, heartbreaking pain, and an unrelenting enemy before, and I am still standing. I know I will face them all again. Potential and purpose don't exist without the presence of pain, and they exist in spite of the presence of pain. The story of my life is a testimony of how joy was found along a troubled path. It is a story of finding purpose through pain.

THE DEVIL OUTSIDE DOING PUSH-UPS

We all want to be successful. We all want to be healthy, strong, and secure. When a new day comes, and the sun rises, we want to experience all of the good it has to offer. We want it all. Good exists in this world and it is available for us. As we dream and strive for all of these things, we need to acknowledge the devil outside doing push-ups. There are real obstacles, pains, and enemies out there. We know what we want, so we need to understand what we are up against. "The devil outside doing push-ups" is an illustration of this reality of life that nothing comes easy or for free.

He is always out there, waiting for us. He wants to tear us down and beat us up. This is our adversary, our opponent in our climb to reach our goals. It doesn't matter what we do, and he is always out there in the parking lot doing push-ups. He sets up obstacles for us. He places temptations in our path. He reminds us of our past pain and failures. He taunts us with doubts and fears. He is always ready, always prepared. Neither you nor the devil knows exactly what is in store for the day, but his goal is to knock you off your feet one way or another. The only thing on his calendar is going toe to toe with you.

We make our best plans for tomorrow and the next season of life, but the devil is outside making his own plans. There is a classic song lyric from OutKast about this, "…you can plan a pretty picnic, but you can't predict the weather." This is true for each of our lives. We need to understand this challenge and truly embrace the reality of it. We cannot control the circumstances around us. The devil has a way of throwing punches at us when we least expect it. So, we need to start expecting it. There is every opportunity around us, there is potential and purpose in each of us, and there will be obstacles, pain, and enemies along the way. The question is, how are you preparing yourself to avoid obstacles, pain, and enemies when you can and overcome them when you can't?

You and I are different. We have had different experiences and have lived out a different story. There is no sense in comparing success and failures, nor comparing how high each of us has climbed up in life. The journey is unique for each of us, and the opportunities and obstacles are unique as well. If life is a mountain of infinite depth and infinite height, then it doesn't matter how high or how successful you appear. The devil doesn't care how much money you have, what your title is, or what car you drive—he just wants to rob you of your joy and purpose. Purpose and joy come from moving forward day by day, season by season. Life really has infinite potential in both directions. The devil wants you to know it can always get worse so you live in fear. He wants you to doubt things could not get any better so you live in complacency. He wants you to believe who you are and what you have isn't enough so you are paralyzed by doubt.

This is why you shouldn't compare your life, your pain or purpose, with anyone else's. Life is a journey with problems to solve, lessons to learn, but most of all, experiences to enjoy. Comparing your life to anyone else robs you of your joy and your own journey. The devil will taunt you with someone else's pain to minimalize your own, stopping you from processing or dealing with it. The devil will taunt you with someone else's success to minimalize your own, stopping you from celebrating and appreciating your own.

Here is a hard truth—you are going to screw up, you're going to trip and fall, and you are going to fail. I just wanted to tell you it's okay; that's life. We all go through it. We all struggle at times. The devil outside wants us to fail, but he really wants us to be too afraid to try. The key to navigating life is not avoiding pain or failure. It is having the tools and the ability to move through them. When you fall, you need to pick yourself back up. Then you can use those moments to learn, grow, and develop accountability. So, stop viewing pain or failure as a dead end and begin to view them as opportunities for growth and potential.

In countless ways, the devil is in the parking lot doing push-ups, waiting for his chance to try and kick your ass. The journey of life comes with many obstacles, pains, and an enemy. As we journey through my story, I hope you see my lowest moments and know despite all of the pain, my purpose remains. As we dive into the four quadrants of success, my hope is you are encouraged and challenged by the lessons I have learned so you can be prepared to face life with more confidence and joy. The devil outside doing push-ups is our metaphor for our external reality, the truth of a broken world. "The story we tell ourselves" is our metaphor for one of our biggest internal struggles.

THE STORY WE TELL OURSELVES

To be honest, this is a book I never thought I would write. First of all, I was not sure I could write a book. Like most new experiences and opportunities, the questions and unknowns can sometimes turn into doubts and fears. Have you ever had the thought or inspiration to do something new? Have you ever aspired to achieve something great? And have you ever felt the presence of negative energy or emotions weigh down your potential? Have you ever talked yourself out of achieving your dreams? You are not alone. Every single one of us has experienced some form of self-doubt or roadblock in our life.

Writing a book is a great example of this. According to a *New York Times* article, 81 percent of Americans want to write a book and publish it for the world to read. There are many different reasons for writing a book, and certainly different stories to tell and information to share, but that is still a whole lot of people who want to write a book. Think about that number for a moment. The percent totals out to hundreds of millions of people, all with one common goal. And, of all those people, only 1 percent will actually write a book— only 1 percent.

So, what does this information tell us? Millions of people have a book inside of them, but only a small portion goes the distance, crosses the finish line, and publishes it. Each of us has a purpose. Each of us has potential. A world full of opportunity awaits you. However, the devil is outside doing push-ups. There are obstacles and pains that get in our way. But it isn't just external circumstances or forces working against us! We also have an internal struggle with the negativity and doubt we face inside of our hearts and mind. The story we tell ourselves can often be the biggest obstacle we face in finding success and living out our purpose.

- "That is good for someone else, but I'm just not cut out for it."
- "I might as well quit now; I know it isn't going to happen."

- "I want to feel better and move better, but changing habits is just too painful."
- "Nothing ever changes. This is as good as it gets."

Have you ever told yourself one of these statements? Perhaps you never said it out loud, but I believe we all have wrestled with similar doubt. Your daily experience is made up of so much more than external forces and circumstances. Whether we realize it or not, we are continually influenced by the story we tell ourselves. Writing a book was not really on my radar because I was living under the assumptions of my story, under the limits of the story I was telling myself. It took a great friend of mine telling me I could do it to spark belief inside of me, and is when the story I told myself began to change.

- "I don't know how," became "I can figure this out. It is worth learning."
- "No one cares, I'm not famous or anything," became "My story is worth telling, and if it impacts one person, then I'll be glad I did it."
- "I have ADHD and I'm already really busy," became "I know I can be disciplined and dedicated with my time, energy, and focus."

The story we tell ourselves is a powerful tool for building ourselves up or tearing ourselves down. What we choose to believe about ourselves will often shape what we really become. There are real obstacles, pain, and an enemy out there in the world—the devil is outside waiting for us—we don't have much control over that. When the phone rings and we hear a voice of negativity and doubt, we often want to blame it purely on the devil as well, but that call is coming from inside the house. Too often, we let the obstacles and chaos around us become our own internalized beliefs about ourselves and our future. When we do this, we are placing ourselves in a box, trapping ourselves with perceived limitations.

Our actions and emotions always originate from pictures and stories playing in our hearts and minds. When we can grasp on to the hope of our purpose and potential, then we begin to tell ourselves a greater story. When the story we tell is limited to the circumstances of our past or present, then our future will remain unimaginative and limited. It is easy to make assumptions about ourselves; it is easy to limit our purpose and potential to the things that have been done to us or said about us. The trauma and pain we face are very real, but so is our purpose. The key to facing each day, to beating the devil outside waiting for us, is to tell a better story. Think outside the box of your past experiences. Live beyond the measure of your sight. Believe in a better story.

One of my kids is going through a phase of loving unicorns and rainbows. I love the variety of conversation topics I get to explore every day. I seriously never know what I'm going to hear or end up talking about. So, I'll let my daughter's passion inspire the words for this point: life isn't all unicorns and rainbows. You already know that, but you need to hear it again. We all do. Life is not simple, and life is not fair. No one can predict the future or assure you of the weather.

Life comes in seasons and waves. Ever-changing. Always shifting and never staying the same. As I mentioned earlier, I can feel the transition of a new season coming. I've been riding a large wave with some sudden dips and some surprises, but for the most part, it has been smooth. I want to clarify each moment carries weight; each day is a season in itself, a cycle. Any collection of moments, days, months, or years can become a season. The key is to understand nothing is ever guaranteed to stay the same. Each cycle has a probability of new success or new failure. The biggest mistake we can make is assuming things will not and cannot change at any moment. That is when we stop growing, stop climbing, and stop telling a better story.

I'm not sure how you're feeling right now, but I'm sure there have been times when you've felt weary, discouraged, and defeated. Don't worry—you're not alone. There is a life of deep meaning, adventure, beauty, courage, and intimate relationships out there. There is a life and a future for you if you're willing to fight for it. It is out there, it is available, but it isn't cheap, it isn't easy, and it isn't quick—but it's worth it. That's why I wrote this book, to offer my story and experiences as hope and encouragement to those who might be discouraged and to challenge you with insights and steps to achieve greater success. These things are possible for you and anyone you share your life with. There are no guaranteed outcomes or results, just guaranteed potential and purpose.

TAKEAWAYS & GROWTH QUESTIONS

This first chapter is setting up some pins for us to bowl through, and we will strike them down again and again throughout the book. You will see these phrases and ideas echo and repeat in the chapters ahead. The key takeaways from this chapter will change your life if you dive in and apply them to the past, present, and future.

1. Your life holds limitless potential and purpose.
2. There are external forces beyond your control, a source of obstacles and pain.
3. The story you tell yourself determines your focus and direction.

The next chapters of this book will dive into my story, but before we get there, let's work through some growth questions. These questions are an extra opportunity to think and process through the content of each chapter. You can take a quiet moment to answer these by yourself, and perhaps you'd like to write your answers down so you can come back to them later. If you feel comfortable, I will encourage you to answer these questions with a friend, spouse, or small group. Living and growing don't have to be solitary acts. In whichever way you feel is best, answer these questions:

1. What do you think about the first key takeaway, "Your life holds limitless potential and purpose?" What is your reaction to this statement?
2. What would living a day full of purpose look like for you? If you are, that's awesome!
3. What external forces, pains, and circumstances are you up against at the moment?
4. What is the story you're telling yourself? Where is your story headed? If you could write the next chapter of your story today, where are you going next, and what will you do?

chapter two

THE UNIMAGINABLE

"WE ARE NOT COMPARING SCARS; WE ALL HAVE
FELT PAIN. SOMETIMES, THE WORST THING
HAPPENS, PAIN CREEPS IN, AND THE UNIMAGINABLE
HAPPENS. AND EVEN STILL, THE PURPOSE REMAINS.
WE ARE MORE THAN THE PAIN WE EXPERIENCE."
JUSTEN ARNOLD

WE ALL STARTED SOMEWHERE

I love getting out into the woods, walking, and hiking through the trees. Especially in an older forest, a place where you know the trees have been around for a long time. I wonder what they have seen, what they have experienced, and what stories they could tell. It amazes me to imagine at one time, each of those trees started out like a seed. At one point, this humongous tree, this immovable object, was a tiny and vulnerable sprout. It looks so strong now, but

I know from its beginning until now, there have been many winters, droughts, and storms. This tree has arrived. I'm seeing it now in the place and form it was meant to be. But I know it hasn't always been like this.

Nothing embodies life or the nature of our journey through it, quite like a tree. Imagine yourself like a tree today, in this season of life. What kind of tree are you? What do you look like, and what kind of fruit do you produce?

Like trees, we don't get to decide where we are planted. We don't get to control the weather or nature around us. As life begins, we put down roots and begin to grow where we are. Season by season, we find more nutrition and strength, while we also face new obstacles. Each of us has gone through cycles of growth, seasons of change, obstacles, and pain. We all started somewhere. We were all once a seed, planted to grow. I'm sure you have seen a tree or plant growing in an unusual place. Sometimes roots break through the foundation of a house or through the sidewalk downtown. I've seen trees in places far from water, high up in the mountains, and on rocky terrain.

Anywhere I see a fully grown tree, I know they did not arrive at this stage because life was easy for them. I understand their branches did not reach these heights because the sun always shined. I understand their roots did not reach their depths because the soil was always soft and welcoming. The trees we see all around us exist despite the circumstances they have faced. Many of them are shaped and scarred by past pains and struggles, but they grew right through them. And because they grew through them, we enjoy their fruit and shade, we admire their bumps and knots, and we celebrate their colors and flowers. Trees are a reminder that hope and determination persist in the presence of adversity. A little sprout will grow through its environments, and it will grow even through the most unimaginable pains and obstacles.

WE ALL HAVE A UNIQUE STORY

I'm inviting you into my past and my pain. As I dive into my story, I don't want to create any sort of "Pain Olympics." There are no gold medals or runners-up in pain.

We all have experienced pain in our lives. No one gets a pass, and no one gets a free ride through life. Each of us is different, but pain and struggle are universal. My life story is unique to me, and while only some people can relate to my specific experiences, everyone can relate to pain and the unimaginable moments life delivers. Life is beautiful and wonderful and full of potential, but there should be no illusions of an easy path or expected outcomes. Have you ever encountered a moment or a season of life that was unexpectedly difficult or unimaginably painful? No one wants that for themselves or their children. We want to experience the best of life and believe the best of life as a child. We all begin life as children, and our story starts with birth.

I read somewhere that the odds of being born are 1 in 400 trillion. I'm not talking about the odds of being born in the United

States, or being born a man or woman, or being born into wealth or poverty. This is simply in reference to you existing as a human being on this planet. Incredible odds if you think about it! What's fascinating is to think about how unique we are. <u>No two of us—not even twins—are born perfectly alike.</u> Sure, we have many similarities and can share common characteristics, but there is only one YOU. This is why I believe we really must embrace our uniqueness, own who we are, and quit striving to be anything we are not. Seems simple enough, right? Just be yourself. Yet far too often, we're fearful of doing that very simple thing.

- We think we'll be judged (don't worry, you will).
- We think people won't like us (don't worry, many won't).
- We think we'll look silly and fail and embarrass ourselves (yep, this will happen as well).

It's impossible to make everyone happy and please everyone. I'm thankful to be surrounded by people who have stepped into who they really are and have reaped the rewards tenfold. From convicted felons to ex-addicts to those who just finally had enough of settling in life, the more these people are real, raw, and relevant, the more they thrive. Stop wasting time being anything but yourself. I don't believe it's a random act that you or I exist. I do believe we are alive to make the biggest impact possible in our short time on Earth.

Be you because no one else can. Be you because everyone else is taken.

TELLING MY STORY

Now I get to be me. I get to take my own advice in celebrating who I am while also sharing how I got here. Today, I am a richly blessed man with a life that I am deeply thankful for. I am finding more joy and satisfaction in my fitness, finances, family, and faith than I ever have. My story is unexpected, hard to believe, and at times hard to stomach. We are not comparing scars; we all have felt pain. Sometimes, the worst thing happens, pain creeps in, and the unimaginable happens. And even still, the purpose remains. We are more than the pain we experience.

For me, it all started in the west suburbs of Chicago. My family was settled in and expecting twins. My mother, in her second trimester, experienced unexpected and unprovoked complications that resulted in the loss of my twin sibling. By the grace of God, I held on and was born in 1981 in Naperville, Illinois. I've been told it was an unusually warm winter day. If you have ever lived in that part of the country, then you understand how rare it is to have warm winter days. You can call it whatever you want, but it was a small miracle I was able to enter a warm and welcoming world.

Life in our home was normal in many ways. Both of my parents worked hard to provide for our family. They worked multiple jobs through different seasons of my childhood. I know that they were doing what they thought was best in providing for us, but it was hard not seeing them while they were working so much. Don't get me wrong, I know they have always loved and cared for us, and they still do. Growing up, it was just a reality that they were working a lot, and my brothers and I were together, with neighbors or friends.

Being the youngest is difficult. I think family dynamics can be fascinating, and I know there is some real psychology in birth order and personalities. As the youngest, I had to rely on the help and care of others. I wanted to know I was loved and worth someone's time and attention. As a small kid, I couldn't understand the responsibility and pressure my parents faced, so I began to form this disdain for work and money because that was what kept my parents away. I told myself I'd rather have a million friends than a million dollars.

Sadly, those friendships were hard to come by. I loved being outside but struggled to find good friends in our neighborhood. When I was four and five years old, I was bullied by some neighborhood kids on our street. They would throw our mail into the storm drain and shove me down there to go get it. They were awful to me, and there wasn't much I could do about it. My dad would intervene when he could, rip them off me when they were beating me up. He even called the police a couple of times. At the same, I had a family member that would beat me up and pick on me as well. It was tough out there.

Soon after these incidents, my family invited our friend's teenage son to come over and babysit me and some other family members. This is where the biggest pain of my life really begins. This is where the unthinkable starts. My mother and father were working and doing what they believed needed to be done for our family by working and providing a babysitter to watch us. It is something other families do too. Who hasn't invited a friend's teenage son or daughter to watch their kids at some point?

This guy was a babysitter for our family for over a year while I was five and six years old. I couldn't begin to tell you precisely when it started, but this person who was supposed to care for and protect us began to take advantage of us. I am not the only person affected or molested by this person, but I will only speak to my experience. He began grooming me by putting his hand on my leg. He would take me away from my other family members and bring me downstairs. I remember the brown couch he used to sit me down on while he would look at pornography. He showed me the pornography, trying to normalize what I was seeing. I will not give any details as to what would happen next. Use your imagination if you must—whatever your assumption has most likely happened. This went on for a long time.

DEALING WITH THE UNIMAGINABLE

From four to six years old, I was bullied and beaten by neighbors and a childhood family member while I was also being molested by a teenage boy. While this was all going on, I completely shut down. I did not fully understand what was happening to me or why it was happening. I certainly did not understand how or when to talk about it. None of us did. As I said, I was not alone in the abuse, and my other family members did not tell my parents, the babysitter's parents, or anyone else while this was going on. Around other people,

I shut down and did not speak, which is hard to believe if you know me now. You couldn't get me to shut up if you tried. Trust me, I love talking now and have to discipline myself to let others join in on the conversation because I could keep on going if you let me!

Back then, I was getting ready to start the 1st grade in elementary school. Due to my nonverbal tendencies and general disassociation, I was placed with special programs and activities. This, of course, further fueled those around me who were inflicting pain. I know at least one of my bullies, my family member, was dealing with their own abuse by the babysitter just like I was. But unfortunately, they may have been taking their pain out on me. When we don't confront the source of our own pain, we are often doomed to let it spill out on the people around us. We were all young and trying to deal with something terrible. At home, I was crushed with fear and anxiety, thinking about the next time that babysitter would come over. At school, I was resigned to silence, even though I scored exceptionally high on intelligence testing that they gave me. I was not equipped to handle what was happening around me. It was so evil and so unexpected; we did not have any guards up against something like this.

We all enter into this world as a blank slate. An empty canvas to be filled with rich experiences, connections, and adventures. My life took an early turn in the worst direction. Things would not get better immediately. In fact, it will get worse before it gets better. I cannot change what happened to me back then, but I wish I could tell myself some things, so many things. Obviously, I would tell myself to talk to my parents or the police immediately and end this nightmare. But I would still be dealing with the pain of what happened. For that, I want to start with the truth and encouragement that I am still loved and worthwhile, despite what has happened. The way I felt back then, is not how I'll feel forever. Better and happier is closer than you can see. Life isn't going to get easier, but you are going to get stronger. Don't run from your pain. Push through it, and it will never control you.

Now, I know unimaginable pain is possible. The worst thing can happen and tragically does happen to some. I also know I can get through it because I have. I know I can be loved and valued because I am. I have faith in myself and faith that God has put me here for a reason because I am living in my purpose and growing in my potential. We are not the sum of the bad things that have happened to us. I want you to hear that now because my story does get worse. More pain is coming. This is not a "woe is me" story. This is a look at how strong we can be when we become rooted in what is fundamentally true about ourselves. Pain comes in heavy winds and beating waves, the devil is outside doing push-ups, and we are more exposed to the unimaginable than we ever want to admit. And yet, the sun will rise in the morning, and we will still be here. We don't have to carry our pain or run from it. We need to confront our past and push through it. We have to be willing to lean into the trauma we have been dealt with in order for us to completely come out stronger, wiser, and braver human beings. Rich experiences, connections, and adventures are still out there for you. While it might be hard to fathom at times, you do have the capacity to live a limitless life of purpose through your pain.

TAKEAWAYS & GROWTH QUESTIONS

My story is just getting started. It is shocking and will continue to take some unexpected and unimaginable turns. Again, my heart in sharing my story is rooted in the hope each of us will feel comfortable sharing our own story and embracing the unique life we each have. Thank you for allowing me to share my experiences and my heart with you. There are several fundamental ideas from this second chapter we need to consider and explore. Take some time to review these key takeaways and consider how they apply to your life.

1. Like trees, we must live and grow through different seasons of life. We cannot control where we begin, but we are invited to grow beyond our surroundings.
2. There is only one "you," so embrace who you are and don't try to be anyone else.
3. We will all experience unexpected pain. This might not sound like the most comforting notion, but truthfully it is important to believe we are not bound or limited to the things that do or don't happen to us. We are more than the pain we experience!

The third chapter is going to take some wild twists and turns, but before we get there, let's work through some growth questions. These questions are an extra opportunity to think through and process the content of this chapter. You can take a quiet moment to answer these by yourself, and perhaps you'd like to write your answers down so you can come back to them later. If you feel comfortable, I will encourage you to answer these questions with a friend, spouse, or small group. This is a sensitive chapter, and sexual assault is a deeply painful and personal subject. Don't be afraid to have a conversation with trusted friends and family. Practice wisdom and care for yourself as you take some time to answer these questions:

1. If your life is like a tree, then how would you describe your tree as it stands today? What does it look like, how is it growing, what kind of fruit does it bear?

2. What are some characteristics and qualities about yourself that are unique or most enjoyable to you? There is only one "you," have you ever struggled to want to be someone else?

3. Have you ever experienced an unexpected pain or unimaginable moment in your life? How did you first respond to that circumstance or season of your life? If you have had more time to grow through it, what would you tell yourself back then?

4. Who do you feel comfortable talking to about your life, whether it is celebrating success or processing through pain?

If you are struggling to answer, what steps could you take to expand the number of people you can talk to?

chapter three

HOUSE ON FIRE

"EVERY DAY WE HAVE DECISIONS TO MAKE,
AND IN EVERY DECISION, WE ARE EITHER
CREATING OR DESTROYING... THINKING THIS
WAY WILL GIVE YOU A NEW PERSPECTIVE."
JUSTEN ARNOLD

WHERE THERE'S SMOKE, THERE'S FIRE

I was confronted with unimaginable pain at an incredibly vulnerable stage of life. To be four, five, and six years old and to have physical, sexual, and emotional abuse; it is a deep and scarring pain. There was trouble in my life, trouble in my home, but no one saw the signs. I will not blame anyone in particular, but perhaps it was more of a cultural issue in and around my home, neighborhood, and school. There were things that needed to be done, and everyone was focused on the task at hand. No one had their eyes up to see what was actually happening, or what the real problems were.

We needed money, so my parents worked and worked and worked to provide for our family. They were focused and dedicated to making ends meet. My family needed childcare and babysitting, so people stepped up to watch us. They were focused on meeting the need of supervision, not as much providing care or attention. One family offered their teenage son as a babysitter, our abuser. They, too, were too narrow-minded to see the pain inside their son, let alone notice the kind of devastation he was bringing with him everywhere he went. And the school gave me attention as a child who would not speak, but in addressing that need, they missed the underlying cause entirely.

There is a reason this phrase, "where there's smoke, there's fire," exists. There are often signs and warnings that something is wrong before it all burns down. When there are clear symptoms, there is often an underlying cause. We can either be too distracted to see the smoke or too busy to figure out where it is coming from. Providing for your family, providing childcare, providing education, and special needs programs—these are all great things. However, we have been living in a culture of busyness and tunnel vision. We are too distracted to see the problems going on around us, and we are too busy to treat anything other than the symptoms. I can't help but think of the people who had the opportunity to pause and evaluate what was going on, to dig deeper into why I wasn't talking, to look further into who this kid was and what types of behaviors he was exhibiting. But no one did.

I am not bringing this up to cast further guilt or blame on anyone else. I want to point out something that is important for you and me to consider as we continue to grow, lead, and love throughout life. There are a lot of very good things begging for our full attention. There are a lot of very important things demanding our time. We are invited to tell ourselves that the most important thing is to provide, meet a need, and take care of a symptom. We are tempted to believe we just don't have the time to work and be present with our spouse or kids. Or we cannot exercise or change our diet because it costs too much money. Important things don't have to come at the expense of everything else. That is a limiting mindset, and the story we are telling ourselves is too small and too narrow. Our priorities need to be clear; our goals need to be founded on our purpose; our success should never come at the expense of care for ourselves or others. There is a healthy way to pursue purpose, potential, and success with balance and care. We will get into that in the later chapters of this book. For now, back into my story.

GETTING OUT

There were three of us. Two child-aged family members and I were being watched by a predatory teenage babysitter. I won't speak for anyone else, but I can say that I could not have been treated any worse than I was during this time. We were not able to communicate to anyone what was happening to us. I know that I was unable to speak to anyone, let alone accuse and confront my abuser. However, things could not go on like this forever. Eventually, someone would find out and there would be hell to pay.

This had been going on for a while, and we were slowly getting older. I was the youngest and did not talk much, so I was the least threatening. The oldest family member, the one that would beat me up and pick on me, well he was getting older and bigger and presented the biggest threat. This had to have been weighing on the mind of the babysitter, and he must have started getting more and more nervous that he would be found out and paranoid that the oldest child would rat him out. So, he devised a plan, an evil and stupid plan that he hoped would set him free from his sins. I don't know how long he had been planning it, if he was waiting for the right moment or if it came to him suddenly. Either way, the day finally came when he made his move.

Both of my parents were working, and the three of us were home with the babysitter. He moved about our house, tinkering with a few things and grabbing a few supplies. He heated up our family's iron and he placed it on the carpet. Our home slowly began to fill with smoke, and then a fire started in the house while we were all inside. With our house now on fire, he grabbed the second oldest child and me and brought us to our neighbor's house. He wanted to look like a hero for saving us and sounding the alarm that there was a fire. However, he intentionally left the oldest child inside the house. In his mind, we were the younger two kids, and we would be less likely to talk and less credible if we did. The oldest was the biggest threat, so he was left in the house to die in the fire. Saving us and acting like a hero was all part of his act, part of his plan to avoid being found out.

The fire station and police were called out to our home. At this time, my mother was actually working as a guidance counselor and a firefighter in our community. She was on duty at the station when the call came in. The chief knew the address and pulled my mother aside and told her that she could not come on this job. She knew right away that something terrible was happening at home. I could not imagine that feeling as a parent.

This was my home, these other kids are my family, and this monster was trying to take everything away from us. But he failed! The oldest survived and made it out of the fire and house. The first responders secured the scene. And I was ultimately the one who spoke up to say what had happened, to say what had been happening over the past year. Me, the little one who had no voice, exposed him in his lies and his terror. There was no more hiding, no more pretending to be a hero. The truth was out in the open, and the babysitter was found out. I couldn't understand it fully then, but at the moment, I was stronger than I realized. We all were.

CREATION & DESTRUCTION

How do you begin to move on from this? The babysitter was now gone, facing judgment for the terrible things he had done. I won't get into charges or sentencing, and I won't share whether I believe he deserved more or less punishment than he received. The focus now and then was moving on. We can only control what we can control. We are responsible for our actions and reactions, much more than we are responsible for circumstances and outcomes. Each person in my family needed their own time and cared for processing and healing. This would be the start of how we move forward, making decisions one day at a time.

We cannot control everything that happens around us or to us. We cannot always avoid pain; it sneaks up on us in unexpected and unimaginable ways. We do, however, have control over what we do with our daily life. Every day we have decisions to make, and in every decision, we are either creating or destroying. Thinking this way will give you a new perspective.

When you wake up in the morning, does your morning routine create energy and joy and potential in your life, or does it destroy and limit them? When we are getting ready for bed at night, does your nighttime routine create restoration and preparation in your life, or does it destroy it? Think about conversations with your spouse or kids and how our words are either building or cutting. Consider your calendar and daily schedule, it could be building you up, or it could be knocking you down. Look at what you eat and drink. How is it helping or hurting your health? Think about actions and reactions at work and how they are either building or destroying customer relationships or productivity. You get the point! Every day, every decision is either creating or destroying. There is not a meaningless decision and there is not a neutral option!

Telling a better story, living out your purpose with unlimited potential begins when we make daily decisions for creation and growth. It can be little steps, adding small disciplines and building layers of hope and confidence one at a time. The devil outside doing push-ups will try to keep you down, to knock down your house of cards and tempt us with destructive alternatives. Don't listen to him! We need to hold on to our identity, our God-given purpose, and take step after step to unleash our limitless potential.

This idea of choosing creation over destruction is especially true in response to pain. When destruction is introduced into our lives, whether by choice or by circumstance, the quickest and easiest response can often be destructive. When we are hurt and angry about things outside of our control, there is a temptation to place our control and pain onto another person. It can become a hellish cycle of pain and suffering that passes from person to person. Or the choice is self-destruction, inflicting more pain on ourselves in the belief that this is the only way to demonstrate control. These are not our only options! These are oppressive lies from an enemy who wants to see the world burn.

Everyone in my family was impacted by this cascading waterfall of trauma. Each of us will have to process the pain we have experienced and make daily choices to either create or destroy in response. Understanding this would have been a game-changer for every single one of us. First, there were missed opportunities for growth and healing that were either ignored or refused. Second, because some of us would not acknowledge the pain that we felt or the potential damage we could cause for ourselves and others. Sadly, some of the worst pain I've ever experienced came in the aftermath of trying to move on from this trauma.

MOVING ON

In order to move forward, my family would need to make a few big choices. We ended up moving to a new house and settling in there. It was nice to have a new place to be, a home that didn't smell like smoke or have the memories attached to certain rooms or spaces. Also, it was great for me to be away from those neighborhood bullies. It was a great fresh start in one area and I'm glad that decision was made. More than the several family decisions, each of us would have countless daily decisions that would guide how we move forward individually. We were all impacted and affected differently, but this happened to all of us and we all had to process our pain in order to move forward.

I'll never forget how angry my mother was after the babysitter was arrested. As a parent, I could only imagine the depth and complexity of the emotions that she felt. Our parents loved us, and they weren't at work all day because they didn't love us. This was a trusted person that was invited into our home and he took advantage of our mother's children. He started a fire in her house and left one of her kids inside. I remember a moment so clearly in my head when we were driving somewhere and my mother stopped the car. She began furiously beating the steering wheel and shouting.

"I'm going to kill him. I'm going to kill him!" she said.

"Who are you going to kill, Mommy?" I asked.

I knew exactly who she was talking about, but I think my little brain wanted to hear her say it. I think it made me feel good knowing that she cared so much and that I wasn't alone in my pain. I honestly didn't want my mom to actually kill this guy, but I took comfort knowing that my parents were on my side and that this monster was never coming back because clearly, they would never let him near me again. And from my perspective, my mom started her journey of moving on and getting herself back to normal.

As for me, I was able to get some psychological treatment, rehab and care after these events occurred. As I was going through evaluations and even some hypnosis, I was starting to speak more. The source of anxiety and fear was gone and I was making daily choices to use my voice more and more. Subconscious or not, it was always my decision to talk or not. After more psych evaluations and even some hypnosis, I was told that I was "fine." That bothers me more now than it did then. At that time, it was a relief to everyone. "I'm fine" was permission to try to move on and forget about it. Looking back, that was a very insufficient response, and more counseling and empathy would have been helpful.

This monster was removed from our life, but his destruction and pain lingered in many ways. We lost so much in the fire: photo albums, favorite toys, keepsakes, documents, and memories. Every time we would look for a photo or birth certificate, it would be a reminder of what was lost in the fire. Some of the furniture that survived the fire still smelled like smoke. It was almost as if our new home was wearing the scars of our last home.

Even still, my family was moving on and it seemed as if the worst was behind us. We were in a new house, both of my parents were back working multiple jobs, and apparently, I was "fine." However, there was one person in my family that wasn't. The oldest child, my family member, the one who would beat me up and was left alone in a burning house—when it was time for him to choose creation or destruction, he chose destruction. He chose to unleash the pain that he felt onto others, especially me. What I am about to share next is devastating, but it is part of my story, so here it is.

For the next two years, I would be molested by a family member. He would isolate me, look at pornography with me, and force me to do things. I can assure you this is very difficult to write. It sounds familiar, though, doesn't it? I suspected that the babysitter did this to him, just like he did it to me, and now this torture was transferring back to me again.

I wanted to move on. I wanted to grow. I wanted to have a normal childhood. They told me everything was "fine." But here I am again, feeling powerless and voiceless, and unseen. This would happen periodically for two years until the other family member, the one who is between us in age, accidentally walked in and caught the older one. The family response was very hushed. I think because we all had been victims, there was a caution to cause trouble or make more pain for the family. It was uncertain what was really happening, and since it was a family issue, it wasn't really brought to the attention of anyone else. He would remain at home. We would be family members, almost like nothing had ever happened. The attitude was just more "you're fine" and hope that everything will be alright.

This would set the path for most of us going forward. Some of us would be leaning into destruction, some trying our best to grow, and others burying their head in the sand and hoping for the best. In a sense, our house was still on fire, and we were all stuck living in it. **For me specifically, this is where I began to have identity issues, trust issues with men, and I would form more relationships with girls; I would continue to feel unseen and unheard.** There wasn't a lot of hope around me, so it was hard to find anything to hold on to. From here through high school, I would wander through life, moving without much inspiration.

REFLECTIONS ON THE PAST

I want to jump in here with some hope and positivity. I decided to share these stories because I know I am not alone in experiencing trauma and pain. I've said several times that we are not comparing or competing when it comes to our pain. We all have experienced pain, and you need to know you are not alone. Also, many of us experience trauma and pain from our childhood. I know I'm not alone. So many of us experienced similar physical, sexual, or emotional abuse. These are raw spots in our heart and mind, and they are moments that have shaped many of our emotions and decisions and actions—especially when we are not conscious of it or acknowledging it.

Writing this book has caused me to remember and relive some things I had not confronted in a very long time. While I wanted to get angry and upset, to blame anyone and everyone for what happened to me, I honestly found relief and light in the end. I am not giving power to these experiences by keeping them a secret and holding them close to my heart. I started by talking with professionals and loving friends and family. It was one of those dear friends who encouraged me to take the step to share my story in this book. Growing day by day, choice by choice, I am now sharing my trauma in order to help and support others who have also gone through pain. Sharing my story has become medicine for me. It is helping me continue to heal after all of these years. I can feel more empathy for everyone, I can offer more forgiveness to those who have hurt me, and I can embrace who I am more and more each day.

We are not defined by the worst things that have happened to us. We are not condemned by another person's choice to hurt us. I was brought into another person's cycle of pain, but I chose to get out and let the cycle die. This doesn't make me a superhero. It doesn't make me better or stronger than anyone else. It only makes me more whole and content being myself and not limiting myself to the pain someone placed on me. Today, I am standing up for the small childhood version of myself. That part of me is still there inside of me, the little sprout turned into a tree. I will always carry him because he will always be a source of creation or destruction inside of me. I can never ignore the little kid who spent those years feeling unseen and unheard by many—now is not the time to ignore him. I'll come back around to this idea later on, but I do encourage you to begin embracing and supporting the parts of you that have experienced pain.

As a victim of sexual assault and childhood abuse, I see you and embrace you. For a moment, I will speak specifically to the men. The current estimations is 1 in 6 boys and men experience sexual assault or abuse. You are not alone. You can begin to heal and when you are ready, you can share your story with the right person until you can share it as a source of encouragement and hope for others. For those looking for some steps, I encourage you to start with a counselor or therapist. Also consider a trusted pastor, family member, or friend. I encourage you to talk to your younger self, give some grace and encouragement to the part of you that has been hurt. If you are finding unchecked and unresolved pain in your past, don't let it sit and rot. Find some help and move towards it. You can create and choose to grow, no matter what the past looks like.

TAKEAWAYS & GROWTH QUESTIONS

This was a tough chapter for me to write. As shocking and as broken as my story is, I hope you have found some insight and encouragement in it. You are not alone, and you can find purpose through your pain. No matter what the past holds, your future is filled with limitless potential! Here are the main takeaways from this chapter. Please add in any other takeaways you have and please send me your thoughts or insights as well.

1. If there is a small but growing sign of trouble, don't ignore it. It takes work to confront pain and obstacles, but it is so much better than letting things burn out of control.
2. You have the power to create or destroy. The choice is yours. While you cannot control everything that happens around you, you are responsible for what you do with your pain and with your purpose.
3. Don't ignore the unresolved pain of your childhood. Your younger self is still inside of you and you need to be reminded you are seen, heard, and loved. Don't bottle your story up or hide it from the world. Even finding one trustworthy person to talk to makes a huge difference.

Take some time to wrestle with these questions. Several of them lean into personal disciplines and daily decisions. I encourage you to take a good look at your daily habits and find some accountability for growth. The decision to create or destroy is yours, including whether or not you take the time to evaluate these questions or skip over them:

1. What are your thoughts on the phrase, "Where there's smoke, there's fire?" Has this ever been true in your life? If so, how was that situation handled?

2. Have you ever felt like you were unseen and unheard? How does that feeling impact and affect you?

3. What are some daily habits you currently have that create energy, joy, and satisfaction in your life? What are destructive daily habits you need to work on? Overall, what is one new choice and habit you can add that will help you grow?

4. Have you ever experienced a cycle of destruction or pain? Has someone ever hurt you because they were feeling hurt?

chapter four

A ROOTLESS TREE

"LIFE IS A JOURNEY WITH PROBLEMS TO
SOLVE, LESSONS TO LEARN, BUT MOST
OF ALL, EXPERIENCES TO ENJOY."
JUSTEN ARNOLD

WONDER

I remember being fascinated with magic when I was younger. In fact, it's all I wanted to learn and study. So, I asked for magic books one year, and I got them! I remember spending hours each day, trying to learn and do every single trick in the book. Maybe part of me wanted to magically whisk myself away from the life I was in to create a mental escape from where I was at. I felt so great when I learned a new trick. I'm not sure how much I could do today, but back then, I was ready to host my own show in Las Vegas! Either way, I am fascinated by magic and magicians to this very day and find joy in the illusions and wonders they perform.

I love that moment where they do something you feel is impossible! Your eyes cannot believe what they saw, and you actually feel conflicted in your mind about whether magic is real or not. It is a childlike wonder, a curiosity that expands the universe of possibilities. Anything can happen if magic is real! But then the performers exit the stage. The show ends, and the audience files out. Or the digital video you have streaming on your television starts to roll its credits. The wonder fades.

Childlike wonder is a gift from God. Kids have this way of problem-solving that blows my mind. I will ask my kids what they think about something and how they would solve a problem. Their answers can range from mythical, mystical, and mathematically improbable—but that doesn't stop them at all. This is the pure joy and imagination of seeing a cardboard box and declaring that it is, in fact, a spaceship or a food truck. Childlike wonder doesn't just give amazing answers, it comes fully stocked with amazing and absurd questions. Kids want to know what this is, why this is happening, how something works, and when we are going to be there. Baked into the chaotic energy is a combustible level of anticipation. Something great is always around the corner, and kids can't wait to get their hands on it.

We obviously don't need to regress to childlike behaviors. Don't go into work and play "the floor is lava," or set your desk up as a pillow fort, or release animals in the Human Resources office.

Actually, all of those things sound like a lot of fun! But, we shouldn't do that. There is a huge difference between being *childish* and being *childlike*. Being *childish* often looks like a grown person living with stunted maturity and emotional intelligence; we need to grow beyond that. Being *childlike* often looks like a grown person who hasn't given up on their dreams, someone who sees the best in others and finds limitless potential where others see "ordinary." *Childish* people complain and throw tantrums when obstacles get in their way. *Childlike* people solve problems with hope, joy, and brilliant ingenuity. Life is a journey with problems to solve, lessons to learn, but most of all, experiences to enjoy. Bottle all of that up and you have a deep well of wonder.

I believe I am living in the deep end of wonder right now, and I love it! As you can probably imagine, it wasn't always that way. My childhood, which should have been an abundant source of wonder and discovery, felt very limited. It felt as if someone kept putting a lid on the well and blocking my attempts to reach in and fill my cup. I was slowly withering away at a time when I wanted to be growing and thriving. I want to share a few more of my struggles and experiences through this time that continue to rob my joy and block my wonder. We are getting closer and closer to when things really start to turn around for me. There will always be pain, and I do love that movie *The Princess Bride* when the guy says something like, "life is pain" and "anyone who tells you differently is selling something." There is a moment when my whole worldview begins to change, and I can truly experience joy and wonder again, even in the presence of pain. We are not there yet. I am sharing this chapter of my story to show you how broken and limited we become when we don't address the pain and the hopelessness we feel.

THAT WILL LEAVE A MARK

As a kid, I wanted to play sports like everyone else. I was struggling with running and would regularly lose my breath. Kind of difficult to play sports when you cannot breathe, right? The doctors said I had childhood asthma and I would need to take medication until I grew out of it. It was frustrating to feel so limited by something that seemed like everyone else does easily, breathing. I didn't really like running for the sake of running, but I liked sports, and I loved being active. As a kid, the pain and discomfort were not enough to stop me from doing the things I liked to do. It hurt, and it drained me, but I wanted to keep pushing through it.

Now, I know kids get hurt, especially when they do some crazy things. I certainly had my fair share of accidents and wipeouts. I was out sledding with my family and several of us were going down the hill together on a sled. The hill was actually at a park that was formed over an old garbage site. The hill was huge and great for sledding, but it wasn't exactly smooth. As we sped down the giant hill, our sled hit something and we came to a sudden stop. I was sitting in the middle and the whiplash launched the person sitting behind me forward into me. Their mouth was open and their teeth sunk into the back of my head. That earned me a trip to the emergency room and some stitches.

A couple of years later, I took a nasty fall at school and that earned me seven more stitches. A few years later, I was in a car wreck. It was wintertime and we had to run two miles home to get help. The next year I tore my rotator cuff. Finally, in my last year of high school, I was in the car on my way to school when we lost control and flipped into a ditch. It was a well-rounded collection of bruises and scars. While I can laugh about these incidents now, I do have to care for my younger self and remember these events took place between the ages of around ten to seventeen years old. All the while, I was dealing with asthma—all the while, dealing with the pain of my past.

FEELING ROOTLESS

I was trying to keep my footing and move forward through all of the pain. What I needed was something to hold on to. A tree holds on by its roots, and that is what my soul desperately longed for. The big question is, where do we find real sources of strength and hope? A growing tree has roots of different sizes sprawling out in different directions. I was trying to establish my roots in many of the typical places: family, fitness, finances, school, relationships, hobbies, health, etc. As you now know more of my story, those potential sources for hope and encouragement were often becoming sources of pain and disappointment. It felt like my roots were either reaching out and finding nothing, or they were being blocked by rocks that were impeding them from growing farther and stronger. Meanwhile, the devil was outside doing push-ups, getting ready to knock me over. Season by season, I was getting older but I was not getting any stronger. I was vulnerable. I felt like a rootless tree.

Now there is a reality, things that are true and are not exactly the same as what I feel. There is and was hope for me; I've always had limitless potential and purpose. I just wasn't seeing it or feeling it at the time. I was looking for purpose inside of my opportunities instead of opportunities inspired by my purpose. Do you see the difference there? I wanted to find my value and my roots in the things around me. You and I don't need a job title to have an identity, value, or roots. You and I don't need to have a certain amount of money, or house, or a car in order to be secure and strong. You and I don't need to have an easy or painless past in order to have a bright and joyful future. Don't identify yourself with your accomplishments or your pain. Both are a shallow and surface-level definition of who you are.

Later on, I would realize my value and my roots are anchored inside of me. I am rooted in what I know to be true about myself and true about the purpose and potential I have—no matter what. At this chapter in my life, I was still stuck believing I was defined by the pain; I thought the obstacles in the way of my roots would never allow me to grow or move forward.

DON'T THROW IT ALL AWAY

In the story of my life, this is not the last chapter that includes pain. However, it is the last chapter that includes pain while I wasn't allowing my purpose to work through it. As I continued to struggle through the teenage years of my life, I was looking for "normal" sources of hope and security. I wanted to have good relationships, but my past traumas made me feel less comfortable building relationships with guys or having any kind of romantic relationship. I was battling some chronic childhood asthma and various injuries over those years, making it hard to feel fully satisfied or secure in my health and fitness. And things at home were still a mixture of pain and conflict between me and the family member who had bullied and abused me.

They were still family, and because I was so young, they were still a part of my life and still had some influence over me. Our family moved again, which brought us closer together and connected us with other family members as well. So, we were all together often, especially around holidays. I remember one Thanksgiving, the same family member who was a source of so much pain and trauma invited me to start doing drugs. He said smoking weed would make me eat more food, and I did love Thanksgiving food, so I tried it. Again, being younger and still looking up to older family members, I ended up being pressured into smoking and selling drugs for a little bit. I acted out and was getting into all sorts of trouble. I would steal sports cards and candy; I was watching some older family members do it, so I would do it too. I finally got caught at a local grocery store swiping some baseball cards and Butterfinger candy bars. All of this was an attempt to be seen and accepted, even by people who were hurting me. I didn't even care about the cards or candy. Many times I wouldn't even eat the candy. It was all a pattern of bad choices I reached for because I just wanted to feel connected to something or someone.

This goes right back to the reality that when we experience pain, we have the choice to either bring creation or destruction into the world around us. This family member, who was about to become an adult and go out into the world, was still carrying the weight and pain of what happened to him. He was still choosing destruction and passing on the cycle of iniquities and pain. At any moment, either of us could make a choice to switch from destruction to creation. You can make that change too! You can rise up and start making daily choices to grow, to tell a different story.

As for me, I was still slowly descending to rock bottom. It finally hit when I lost a couple of family members, a grandfather and great aunt, who were near and dear to me. In school, I had found some hope and strength in the marching band. I was a percussionist and was honestly really good at it. I still love music and drums today. We were traveling on a band trip and loading back onto our bus when a truck driver struck and killed my friend and fellow bandmate. It was heartbreaking. The places where I had looked for identity and hope were just wasting away, and so was I. I began struggling with suicidal thoughts. I felt disgusting, unloved, and unappreciated. I felt the weight of my pain and I did not want to touch it or think about it—the pain was like this heavy cloud weighing down on me but I wouldn't look up at it. I did not have any real thoughts or relationship with faith in God, so it was a struggle to believe in myself or anything bigger than myself.

There were three separate occasions where I made a move to end my life. I didn't see where my story could go next, so the story I told myself was I would be better off ending than going on in pain. I felt fatally flawed and the devil was whispering in my ear that this is all there is, nothing will ever get better. Without much hope, some small voice fought back and stood up at just the right time. Something clicked, a flip switched, and I knew things needed to change. I needed to change.

I wanted to throw it all away, but I also had this notion that hurting myself or ending it all would be the worst thing I could do. So, I stopped trying to throw it away. I did not know how to move forward. I wasn't sure why but I needed to tell a different story. One small thing impacted me was being able to play the drums in the band again after my bandmate had passed away. We got to perform for a parade, and we knew our bandmate's family was in attendance. When we neared their location, I called out a drum cadence that was his favorite, and I called out his name. I was told later how much it meant to his mother, that she cried and smiled as we made this small but special honor to her son. It didn't fully hit me at first, but the seed was planted. I have something to give; I can help someone else who is hurting. Throwing away my life would only bring more pain into the world, even if I felt like no one would care—I knew my family and bandmates would. I knew I would just be taking the pain that was dumped on me and by trying to throw it away, I would just be spreading it all out on everyone else. No, I'm not going to do that. I would much rather provide a small act of encouragement, a small piece of support for someone else who is hurting. Don't believe what the devil is whispering in your ear. You have a purpose, and you have life and love to share with the world around you. No one is better off when we throw it all away.

There are resources out there, counselors, pastors, and support groups. I encourage you to explore them. If you have ever wrestled with the thoughts of throwing your life away or hurting yourself, then you need to catch a new breath and take a step towards your purpose and potential. You may not see it now because you have a heavy cloud over your head, just like I did. You are not alone in this. It is time to start clearing the air and finding a fresh and renewed heart. You have purpose through pain. You have limitless potential beyond what you see or feel. There is only one of YOU in the world, and the world is better with you here.

TAKEAWAYS & GROWTH QUESTIONS

I hope that you found some encouragement and inspiration in this chapter. Once again, this was a dark chapter for me, but I can share this story with so much hope and so much excitement now because of what I know to be true. It is a blessing to be here and I am not going to throw away the life, purpose, and potential that I have. You and I are greater than the circumstances around us. Our value and our roots are not in our outcomes or results. True identity and strong roots come from deep within ourselves. They come from a source that abusers cannot touch, robbers cannot steal, and we cannot throw them away. We are getting closer and closer to the good news, the hope and the chapters where my purpose shines brightly through the pain. First, let's take a moment to review the key takeaways from this chapter.

1. We all need a sense of wonder, hopefulness, and curiosity that pushes us through doubt and pain. Kids are full of it! As adults, we need to be childlike (not childish) in our ability to see what matters the most, and find joy in the world around us.

2. Don't look for purpose inside of opportunities. Instead look for opportunities inspired by your purpose.
   Our identity and value are not rooted in our titles, experiences, or wealth. Don't identify yourself with your accomplishments or your pain, as both are a shallow and surface-level definition of who you are.

3. The future is bright, even if you cannot see it or feel it at the moment. You are not alone, and you can find a qualified and trusted person to help you see past the cloud. You still have purpose through pain. You have limitless potential beyond what you see or feel.

Once again, find time to work through the questions below from this chapter. You can do this individually, with a friend or spouse, or perhaps a small group of trusted friends. These questions are here to encourage you to plant seeds of hope and truth in your life or water them if they are already there. As a gym owner and fitness expert, these questions are like stretches and exercises for your heart and mind:

1. What kind of imagination and wonder did you have as a kid? How does childlike wonder play out or exist in your life now? Can you point to something in your life recently that your younger self would be excited for or proud of?
2. Have you ever experienced something very physically painful? How did you, or do you, react? Do you have any scars from your past?
3. What are your sources of identity, strength, and hope—what do your roots look like? When life gets messy, what or who do you hold on to?
4. Life, purpose, and potential do exist beyond what you can see or feel at times. What is blocking you from seeing a bright future? What obstacles and challenges are limiting the story that you are telling yourself right now?

chapter five

TOXIC MASCULINITY

"BEING A REAL MAN MEANS BEING REAL.
YOU CAN BE VULNERABLE, YOU CAN CRY,
YOU CAN BE WEIRD, YOU CAN BE YOURSELF."
JUSTEN ARNOLD

DIVING INTO THE DEEP END

Alright, I know this is a loaded subject… but let's go there for a moment. Let's take a brief pause in my story, and let's jump headfirst into a hot topic of conversation. First, this book and this chapter are not just for men. This is an open invitation for everyone to read, digest, and even disagree with the words I have to share. Second, let the title of this chapter be what it is without bringing your own definition and assumptions into what I am going to share. I experience this in the gym all of the time. Someone comes in, and we get them into an exercise. I say the name of the movement, and they nod their head with excitement as if they know exactly what I'm talking about. They then go on to do a strange movement that does not at all resemble the exercise that we assigned. People have different definitions and understandings of something, so let's all be careful not to get too far ahead of ourselves or assume that we already know everything that I am going to say. Cool, let's do this!

This chapter is called "Toxic Masculinity." I am a man, so I will speak from my perspective on what I have discovered and experienced. When it comes to finding purpose through pain and unleashing your true masculine potential, I believe there are some unique challenges in the culture and expectations of masculinity. I don't believe masculinity is evil; men are not inherently bad or worse than women. That is a terrible and destructive point of view. I do believe that structures and systems have elevated certain traits and ideas of masculinity in a way that has actually hurt men and society in general. I am using the phrase "toxic masculinity" to represent the thoughts and actions that continue a cycle of pain, stunts growth and development, and tells a limiting story of what a "real" man can be or do.

In this chapter, I want to break down some of these ideas and dive into a deeper and more real nature of masculinity. It is not enough to highlight broken ideas or incomplete definitions. We need to put the pieces back together and be our true selves. Being a real man means being real. You can be vulnerable, you can cry, you can be weird, and you can be yourself.

BE PRESENT

Let's start here, masculinity should include being present for the things that matter most in your life. There is a toxic trait and characteristic in our culture of busyness. Trust me, this is not just an issue for the guys. Everyone is busy, and very few people are present. There is an undercurrent of "Go! Go! Go!" We are constantly busying ourselves with something. The tragic part is we are also becoming more and more busy doing nothing! Our greatest tools and inventions are pressing us to be more and more attentive to what is happening on our phones, pulling us from being present wherever we are, and from whomever we are with.

Being driven is a great quality. Getting things done is a great characteristic. However, if we are not careful, these traits begin to form a toxic habit of always being disconnected from the world around us. I had unresolved tension, emotion, and pain in my life— busyness was an escape for me. If I don't have to be available or still, then I don't have to give my own thoughts and feelings much attention. Pretty soon, the habits of avoidance spill over into other relationships, starting a cycle of pain that begins to impact the people closest to us. I never wanted to make someone else feel like they don't matter. I hated feeling that way. However, there are some cultural aspects of toxic masculinity that invite me to do just that. After all, I'm getting things done, and I'm winning and succeeding and doing stuff. We will dive more into this topic, especially in the chapter on "Limitless Family."

BE VULNERABLE

One toxic trait and perspective on masculinity is the pressure to be guarded and emotionally withholding. It is the old cowboy who holds his cards close to his chest, makes no expression or indication of what he is holding on to. That just might work in a card game, but it is a lonely and repressed way to go through life. At some point, a cultural expectation was established for guys to rarely share what is really on their mind, especially if they are dealing with a past pain or emotional struggle. The idea that men need to be ruggedly stoic and individualistic goes back a long way. It is ingrained in film and legend, heroes who wouldn't blink at an emotion, let alone wear one on their face.

I am not advocating for the far extreme of posting your diary on social media or telling everyone in your barbershop about your deepest darkest fears. Sometimes we argue against a true statement or avoid the conversation by jumping to the wildest conclusions. To be vulnerable is to be real and authentic and to open yourself up to real and authentic relationships. There are some amazing characters from movies and television that portray this kind of self-reliant, overly guarded masculinity. One of the best is a character named Ron Swanson, from the television show *Parks and Recreation*. If you know the show, then you know the character. Ron is often propped up for his blunt and to-the-point responses, his general avoidance of personal conversation, and his professional ambition to never accept a meeting with anyone. What I love about the character, besides being absolutely hilarious, are the moments when he finally opens up and shares his affection for his co-workers and friends, his heart for mentorship and teaching, and his passion for his many crafts and skills. It is rewarding as a spectator because you know that is what he is supposed to do—open up and be vulnerable. It also means that it is possible for the manliest of men to share vulnerable insights into their life with trusted friends. Without those vulnerable moments, Ron Swanson might be a funny character, but he would ultimately be a miserable and lonely one. Whether you have seen that show or not, we can all take our own steps to grow and become more vulnerable.

When men and women cannot be vulnerable, everyone loses. There have been cultures and structures in place that gave the notion that men ought to solely focus on providing, winning, and succeeding—"the emotional stuff is not for us." I want to call out this toxic trait for what it really is, fear. I felt it, and I saw it all over the place. The fear inside of toxic masculinity grabbed a hold of this "men don't talk about their feelings" concept because being vulnerable requires us to be exposed, left to the mercy of those who might hear or see us. I have gone through life not wanting to open up about my story because what would people think about me? I have entered a health and fitness space that is often hyper-focused on superficial results and images; the gym is not what many people imagine as a tender or emotional place to be. Personally, I have found it to be an amazing place for people to open up, share parts of their stories, and build relationships. Throughout my journey writing this book, I've had countless conversations about these chapters—you holding this book right now may even be one of those people!

We do not need to fear our past because our past does not define us. We don't need to fear our future, it does not define us either. The past, present, and future can cause all sorts of energy and anxiety as we process pain and wrestle with the unknowns—that much is very true. So, men would be wise to find counsel, encouragement, and strength by opening up and sharing what they are feeling. Gentlemen, stop holding back, stop being afraid to be vulnerable. With the numbers on sexual abuse in men, you would think that we would hear about it more often. Why don't guys talk about stuff like this? Is it because we are so strong that we can carry it all by ourselves, hold it all in until we explode? No, it's because, at some point, the devil in the parking lot knew he could trick us into carrying the load by ourselves, making us weaker and more isolated than ever. Men need to talk about their thoughts, dreams, fears, and feelings. It doesn't have to all be negative. Get out there and find some accountability partners that will help you get back into a healthy fitness routine, grow in your skills and passion, and achieve your goals.

BE OK WITH TEARS

There is a very famous movie scene and quote that you may have heard before. A man is brought in to coach a women's baseball team, and the movie dramatizes the disparity between a woman's reaction to tears and a man's reaction. The coach, played by Tom Hanks, is making what we are led to believe is his best attempt to work with a weeping female baseball player. The coach yells and berates the player for making the wrong throw. The female player, someone who has gone most of her life being yelled at, bursts into tears. The coach is equal parts shocked and angry to see her crying. He erupts, "There's no crying in baseball!"

He actually goes on to explain to her that she cannot cry because he never cried when he got yelled at. Listen, I'm not trying to ruin a classic cinematic moment here, but this is an important thing to observe because although this is a film, this moment is very much based on the reality of toxic masculinity. You need to watch the movie if you haven't seen it in a while. It is a perfect example of a man who is dealing with emotional and physical pain, both from the circumstances of life and the destructive choices that he made along the way. He continues to choose destruction for himself and those around him, in contrast to these women who have also suffered greatly but ultimately deal with their pain with more poise and strength. This man is so caught up in hiding his feelings, burying his pain, when his female player starts to cry, he actually becomes enraged. I love the movie, but it is a sobering reminder that men being afraid to cry or be around someone who is crying is not a healthy or productive trait.

The avoidance of tears from your own eyes or someone else's is not a sign of strength. It is a toxic movement in human history. I'm not going to make the comparison between men and women, and I'm not saying men and women have to cry at the same time over the same thing. I'm just pointing out that real and authentic people, men and women, have many ways of expressing their pain, joy, and laughter. Tears should always be an option for everyone who is capable of producing them. Crying isn't just for girls.

I can tell you that just about everyone who cries in front of me apologizes for it. Why do you think that is? How did we get to a place where we need to apologize for having emotions and allowing a biological process to take place? Crying should not be taboo, and it certainly shouldn't be shameful. Tears are therapeutic and helpful, it is healthy for you to cry. It is more than a natural process; it is a necessary one. Holding emotions back limits us from future relationships and builds aggression inside of us. Unresolved conflict will build and eventually erupt. I mean, there is a science to crying. To the brain, it's parasympathetic, sending a signal to the glands in the eyes to release tears. Once the emotional purgation is over, the body is able to slow down its breathing and heart rate to a more controlled pace. This entire experience sends a positive release throughout the body and gives off the feeling of relief for the person. It's similar to getting a massage or sitting in a hot tub, or restorative yoga. It feels good, and it is good for you.

If crying is weak, then so is pooping. I dare you to hold that in when your body wants to let it out. Just kidding, don't do that. It is a natural and biological process that is healthy when we do it and unhealthy when we go a long time without it. I know guys who will proudly send photos of a turd that they dropped in the toilet and share it with their friends, but would never share a vulnerable moment or cry in front of their closest friends. Allow your body to do what it naturally is built to do. Dealing with your "shit" doesn't mean holding it all in. Be a man and allow your body to do what it needs to do. And if it isn't happening for one reason or another, then be brave enough to ask for help.

BE A PROTECTOR

There is a toxic idea of masculinity that involves being bigger and stronger than everyone else. There is a notion that the sole purpose for men is to be the provider. I believe that the real intent and calling for fathers, husbands, and men is to be a protector. When we take part in bringing life into this world, our role is to protect it. When we enter a commitment in marriage, our role is to protect the relationship and the person we have exchanged our vows with. When we are a part of a community, we honor the lives of those around us by standing up for what is right and defending those who cannot defend themselves. We can be physically strong, we can bring in the majority of the income, and not be a protector for our spouse, kids, or community.

Protecting is more than providing. It requires greater strength to be measured and patient with children when they are seeking our attention. It demands greater provisions of time and support when our spouse needs something from us. And it requires us to sacrifice ourselves with a willingness to step in and do whatever it takes to make the people around us feel safe. Protectors apologize when they are wrong and seek to make things right. They seek to understand the heart and minds of those closest to them and make a conscious effort to use their strength and position for the good of those around them. Everyone reading this can be a protector. You all have it in you!

BE MORE THAN "FINE"

Guys have a tendency to answer an important question, "how are you doing?" with a short answer like "I'm fine." I am not afraid of backing down from using the term toxic masculinity because there is clearly something in the water, and it is breaking us down. The systems and cultures that prop up isolated, guarded, emotionless men are also pumping out some terrifying statistics for men's health and well-being. I have found statistics stating that men's suicide rates are 3.5x higher than that of women: men are 3x more likely than women to become alcohol and drug dependent. Men are disassociating with busyness addictions in social media, video games, and "success." All of this while the divorce rate in America hovers around 50 percent. Gentlemen, we are not "fine."

I know a lot about not being fine or okay. I am sharing my story and my struggles so that you know I understand that life is hard, and the devil is out in the parking lot waiting to try and kick our ass. This toxic idea that we need to face these things alone, be hyper-independent, and shoulder our pain all on our own—it all has to stop! I work with clients who experience chronic pain, and one thing

I hear is that it'll never get better. Friends, men and women, that is simply not true. The story we tell ourselves matters, we need to be more than "fine."

We need to be free to be ourselves and live out our purpose. Listen, I'm a weird dude, and I love being me. I have a didgeridoo and play it often. I still play the drums and have a set in my house. I am a grown adult who loves to play outside and dance in the rain. I love different forms of art and movement; I've taken dance classes and loved them. I will cry when I'm sad, or really happy, or whenever I just need to. I also have many kickass passions and hobbies like weight training, deer hunting, and beard growing. I would eat venison and elk all day. I don't do anything or not do anything because it is or isn't "manly," I'm just being myself. And I will tell you my story about how the worst possible things happened to me, but I'm still here, and I still have a purpose-filled life and a limitless future. Honestly, I have to stop calling myself "weird" because that idea only comes from a standard that is propped up by fear. You and I are stronger and more courageous than that.

You don't have to be like me or anyone else, just be yourself. Let go of the toxic ideas of what masculinity is "supposed to be" and embrace who you really are and how you really feel. Whether you are a man or a woman, you can be who you are and feel what you feel with no false expectation or toxic culture. As for masculinity, I believe that being a "real man" simply requires you to be real, authentic, and to deal with your stuff—grow through your pain.

TAKEAWAYS & GROWTH QUESTIONS

This chapter was born out of my struggles to do what you just read. My pain and past experiences were a heavy burden, and I needed to do the hard work of growing through them. I was lost and disconnected from my purpose. The toxic ideas and culture of manhood encouraged me to ignore what I was feeling, focus on school or work, and guard myself against being too vulnerable. This was the exact opposite of what I needed then and it would be the opposite of anything that the people around me or I would need in the future. Being present is a gift for my family and for me. Being vulnerable and open to talk is a core value for marriage and relationships. Being myself, enjoying unique experiences and hobbies, is not only a joy to me but also allows me to connect to more people and appreciate the unique qualities and passions they have. This conversation is not an attack on men or masculinity. It is a challenge to the walls that have been put up, the small box masculinity has been placed in. These key ideas and takeaways are meant to make us stronger and more secure in who we really are.

1. It takes more discipline and strength to be present than it does to be busy. Busyness in and of itself is not at all wrong, but it can be a veiled excuse for hiding from pain or looking at ourselves in the mirror.

2. It takes courage and integrity to be vulnerable and cry when you need to. Don't bottle everything up inside until

you explode. It is emotionally and physically beneficial to allow yourself to express your feelings and share them in healthy ways.

3. Grow to love who you are and desire more than just being "fine." Be true to yourself, and you will find greater joy and fulfillment in the days ahead. Deal with the pain and fear that is holding you back.

There are growth questions in every chapter of this book. Each set of questions is an invitation to reflect on and answer the prompts in your quiet time while you are alone, with another person, or with a small group of people. However, if there was a chapter that I would push you to find at least one other person or a small group of people to discuss the questions with—it is in this chapter. This is my challenge for you with these questions:

1. What is your view on masculinity? Have you ever experienced the symptoms of toxic ideas or traits surrounding masculinity, either in your own life or from someone else?
2. In your opinion, what stops us from being vulnerable or expressing how we really feel?
3. In your experience, do men talk about emotional and mental stress or pain? With all of the numbers surrounding abuse, suicide, and divorce—why don't men talk to each other more about these things?

4. How do you feel about crying? If you ever cried in front of someone, how would you want them to react to you? How would you react to a close friend or family member who was crying?

5. What is something unique about yourself that is below the surface of what other people might see or outside of the small box of what some might think you're supposed to be?

chapter six

GOOD NEWS

"NOTHING ABOUT MY PAIN OR STRUGGLES
ARE GOOD, BUT SURVIVING THEM DOES NOT
MAKE ME BAD. I AM MORE THAN THE THINGS
THAT HAPPEN TO ME, AND I AM MORE THAN
THE THINGS THAT I HAVE DONE."
JUSTEN ARNOLD

PIERCING THE DARKNESS

Back to my story, let's pick up where we left off. I was suffocating under the weight of a dark, shadowy cloud. The pain and loss of childhood innocence, the broken bonds of family, the loss of friends and relatives—all fueled the storm that was raining hopelessness and thundering loneliness down on me. I could hardly breathe; physically, I was struggling with asthma, but I was emotionally and spiritually breathless as well. The definition and value of my life appeared to be lost in the darkness.

Each of us has a chapter or chapters in our story that includes pain, frustration, and brokenness. We all experience failure, either by our own hands or by the people, systems, or structures around us. When the storms of life come and rage against us, rootless trees will feel like falling. The darkness can make us doubt ourselves, lose sight of where we are going, and dissuade us from living in our purpose or living out our potential. The gravity of our circumstances can appear as if there is no way to move forward. The devil will insist that there is nothing left to hold on to.

I need you to hear me loud and clear, this is NEVER true! Even on the darkest day, the light shines bright above the clouds. Even after the longest nights, the sun comes up in the morning. All it takes is one step of purpose, one seed to plant and grow, one ray of light to pierce through the darkness. You have a purpose; you have a foundational element in you that cannot be overtaken by any force. In the storms of life, the winds can blow and beat against us, but they cannot overcome our purpose. The darkness around us cannot conquer the light inside of us. We have a source, we have a purpose that can shine through anything that life may throw our way.

THIS CHANGES EVERYTHING

In the midst of my pain, I experienced a ray of hope and truth. I caught a glimpse of joy here and there, little moments when I could witness small acts of care, little sparks of light. I found myself creating moments of hope and impact on others. Something inside of me was ready to be unleashed. What if I, with all my pain and baggage, can still positively impact the life of someone else? What if I can make daily decisions to create joy and hope, to shine light in the lives of others? Maybe I had more purpose and potential than I could see. This idea was planted in my soul, but I still wasn't sure that it was real or possible for me. The world was still heavy and dark, so I began to focus more on listening for hope and looking for the light.

It was the summer before I went off to college, and I already knew my life was about to change. This is a big moment for me, a chance to start fresh and move forward. I just needed to find a way to grow and move around my past. I knew that the struggles of my life could continue to box me in, limit my view of self-worth and strength. I had a glimpse of the light, I needed more of it. I needed to find real hope and truth that would unlock my purpose and unleash my potential. And let me tell you, when I finally found it, I knew—this changes everything!

I encountered a single source of light, a cornerstone of truth that transformed the way I saw myself and the world around me. This was the moment when I first believed and accepted that my life holds a God-given value and purpose. It is held deep inside of me, preserved by the intention of the One who put it there. No matter what has ever happened or will ever happen to me, nothing and no one will ever rob me of my value and purpose. There is no power or pain that can take away the promise of what I'm worth or who God created me to be. Nothing about my pain or struggles was good, but surviving them does not make me bad. I am more than the things that happen to me, and I am more than the things that I have done. The light and love I have found will shine through any new struggle or past experiences.

While the pain doesn't go away and our scars do not disappear, this root of truth remains. As I encountered this for the first time, I wrestled with it (and I still do at times). Nothing that has happened to me changed; the reality of life and the circumstances of my past are just as real and painful as they have ever been. But when I embrace this truth that my identity, purpose, and value are not wrapped up in those things—I know that I can grow through and beyond them. By the grace of God, I will make an impact on the world around me. I will find love and joy and hope no matter what happens—because I'm not defined by what happens to me. When it feels like I have no one to turn to, I now know that I could hold on to God and He would always be there for me.

This is good news! It is the very best news, especially in a world where we all experience pain. Our true purpose and potential come from within. There is a God, He created us on purpose with purpose. You may not believe what I believe about yourself or about God. I hope you accept this invitation to let the seed be planted and grow. Wherever you may fall on the spectrum of belief, let it grow one step towards accepting the truth that you have God-given purpose and potential. Let one ray of light in. No matter what you have been through or what decisions you have made in the past, redemption and hope are available to you right now! God made you on purpose with purpose.

FORGIVENESS

Let's talk about forgiveness. It's such a huge part of finding purpose through pain, and it's very countercultural in society, especially in the realm of toxic masculinity. I was recently listening to this podcast focusing on people who have experienced pain similar to what I've experienced. There was still a lot of anger, and hate, and they could not bring themselves to forgive their abuser. They would rather put a bullet in their perpetrator than see them go free. I certainly understand where that feeling comes from and felt that way before, but I honestly couldn't live like that anymore. I had found peace and strength. The security I felt in knowing that I had purpose gave me the grace to forgive others and forgive myself.

When my purpose, potential, and titles do not come from the people or circumstances around me, then it is easier for me to forgive. Yes, I was wronged, hurt, and abused; this should never have happened, and it is horribly painful to go through. Once I found my core truth and value, I knew that I could be forgiving because no one had robbed me of my purpose. I'm saying this knowing now that it isn't easy, and I know that the pain will resurface throughout my life. So, I will continue to have opportunities to hold on to what is true and move forward. Forgiveness ultimately is an act of moving forward, one step at a time. It may feel like we are letting someone off the hook, but ultimately, we are the ones who get to be freed when we forgive the people who hurt us. Anger and guilt are weights like gravity that pull us down; if we cannot find forgiveness, then our abusers are still holding control and power over us. It is time to begin to grow and find purpose through the pain, it is time to find forgiveness and begin to move forward.

TAGS & TITLE

I'm sorry, but getting your new tags and title for your vehicle is one of the most annoying processes that we must go through. This regular pilgrimage to a DMV office can be a source of frustration, at least in my experience. I'm not blaming anyone who works there, it's just one of those things that always feels a little more difficult than it should be. When everything is done correctly, you are good to go. The title matters the most because it shows what the vehicle really is and, most importantly, who owns it. Cars and people can be misidentified, and titles can become lost or damaged. Finding the correct title with renewed tags is a crucial part of moving forward. Holding on to the right titles with a renewed heart and mind is a crucial part of moving forward through life.

The name and titles we give ourselves are powerful. What titles and classifications have you given the life that is not truly "you?" We might constantly be called or call ourselves "a drunk," "weak," "fat," "a victim." I know that I held the title and classification of ADHD for a long time in a way that convinced me that I was a failure and not smart enough to succeed. When we identify ourselves or others with these things, we are speaking from a limited mindset that only acknowledges current struggle with no future hope. We are putting ourselves in a box. The pain and trauma are very real, but these things do not have the last word in their attempt to claim our identity. We are meant for so much more. We are meant to be transformed and renewed. We have a title that no one can strip away or cover up. You cannot control what other people say about you, but you can control what you say to yourself and what titles you give yourself. Speaking positively to and about yourself will make a difference in your life and keep you secure in your identity.

Don't copy the behavior and customs of this world, but let God transform you into a new person by changing the way you think. Then you will learn to know God's will for you, which is good and pleasing and perfect.
Romans 12:2 (NLT)

EVERYTHING MATTERS

Small things have big consequences! Over time, the seemingly small and daily decisions we make compound and grow. We have accumulated momentum for all our choices. Waking up on time is a small decision that has a ripple effect on the rest of your day. Getting a good night's sleep and eating well: these are a combination of choices and little moments that combine to impact one day at a time. Over the course of many days and weeks, those choices compound and make an even greater impact on your health and wellbeing. I know firsthand how many people believe that going to the gym is a one-time, binary decision: go today or don't go today. However, building a habit of going to the gym or expecting to see results requires more than a one-time decision. Do not be the person who thinks showing up one time and doing some curls is going to give you bigger biceps. I wish it worked that way, but it doesn't. Each daily decision matters as they all influence the trajectory and potential of your long-term growth and health. Trust me, real fitness and health are not achieved in a single day or single decision. Each moment holds potential; everything matters.

Purpose is an ongoing pursuit, a lifelong journey. We can use our daily decisions to live our purpose and unleash our potential. It may not feel like we are doing a lot when we set our phone down and go to sleep at a reasonable time. It may not feel like we are changing the world when we go on a walk with our family. These little moments make bigger impacts than we immediately see. And they are ultimately setting a course for where our life is headed. We have all experienced major decision points in life before. These decisions come up every so often, and they are milestone moments in life surrounding education, marriage, career changes, housing, finances, faith, and health. We all understand the weight of those big decisions, but we underestimate the value and importance of our daily decisions and habits.

The good news is that we have control over our decisions and our habits. We can set our sights on purpose-filled goals and aim to unleash our limitless potential on the world around us. No matter what steps out into our path, we can navigate our lives through any opposition or force, or pain. The good news is that when we feel helpless, our daily decisions matter and they make a bigger difference than we realize. We can take control and set our course by making our moments count. We also have the good news of knowing that no matter how out of control or destructive our habits have been in the past, there are steps for us to take to turn around and head in the other direction. If you do not know where to start, look for the most practical and available opportunity to grow and start there. Find someone who is living in their purpose and ask them for advice or mentorship. Trust that God is on your side and take a step. We are all learning and growing together. Your time and effort mean something. Start where you are and move one step at a time—everything we do matters. Everything we do can make a difference.

FIGHTING BACK

I was hoping to head off to college with a fresh start, and, wow, I got one! My life was not fixed or pain-free, but I realized that it was never as broken or hopeless as I thought. I'd walked through hell for years, but I no longer needed an escape. I am content with who I am and who I believe God is. It doesn't remove the pain, but it allows me to grow through it. The obstacles around me had not gotten smaller or weaker. I was growing bigger and stronger.

I was setting myself on a course to live life to the fullest, no matter what might be thrown my way. When I went off to college, I would do a lot of great things, I would continue to play percussion at a high level (I still play the drums and love it), I would begin to study health and movement, and I would grow to believe more about myself and what I'm capable of. I would get into theatre and dance, and I would go on to minor in dance as part of my degree. I hid that from some people for a while still, fearful of being ridiculed for that. Now I'm excited and open to talking about the benefits and lessons of dance and how it strengthened my body and mind.

My purpose inspired me to begin using my time and testimony to encourage and support others. Once at college, I became highly involved with HEAT, the Health Education Advocate Team. HEAT was an organization that provided presentations and educational events about rape, sexual assault, and healthy relationships. I was growing and healing. I wanted to fight back against the terrible things that happened to me by being a light in the darkness for others. From this point on, my life's struggles have been a tool for providing hope and healing. What was only intended for evil is now a part of doing good.

We've touched on revenge and forgiveness already, but let me end with this. Any action or thought of getting back or getting even by perpetuating pain is wrong. No one is better and no one is healed when the pain returns. The best way to fight back against darkness and pain is to change the world with light and hope. Joining a group like HEAT was a blessing for me and a blessing to those who were encouraged through the presentations and information. You do not have to get up on a stage or share your story with anyone. You just have to find a way to be a light for those who need it. Then, everyone wins.

TAKEAWAYS & GROWTH QUESTIONS

This is a chapter of good news. My life hit a turning point when I encountered the truth of who I am. The strength and the certainty of being rooted in my God-given life and purpose changed everything for me. I believe what I believe, and I hope you know that I have no judgments or expectations for you. I've said it before, and I'll say it again, my hope is that your beliefs about yourself and about your God-given purpose will grow just one step forward. I was ready to throw my life away because my past pain and trauma told me that I was worthless and abandoned. Once I realized that wasn't true, I turned my back on the darkness and embraced the light. You will see in the next chapter that the darkness would still scream and hit and pull at me, but it will never own my identity or purpose. Take a moment to review and reflect on the key takeaways from this chapter.

1. It just takes a sliver of light to remember that there is more than the pain and darkness around us. Once we accept the light and purpose inside of us, we will realize that we are more than what happens to us or around us.

2. Our purpose and identity are solid and unbreakable. We need to renew our hearts and minds and keep our title fixed on what is most true about ourselves. We are more than the labels or titles that the world offers us.

3. Everything we do matters and can make a difference. Our daily decisions influence our direction in life. Our good news can be shared and make a difference in the world around us.

Take some time to go through these growth questions. As always, you have several options for how you can work your way through them. Be honest with yourself and the people you may be sharing your thoughts with. The choice is always yours; choose to be authentic. If you have your own questions, then add them to your reflection and discussion! Here are the questions I'm offering for this chapter:

1. Have you ever experienced hope and encouragement from someone else when you were going through a dark moment? What did that look like, and how did it make you feel?

2. Do you believe that you have innate value and purpose? If not, what is holding you back from accepting it? If you do, where does that belief come from?

3. What competes for your identity the most—what person, quality, or function is most often associated with you? What words do you most often use to describe who you are?

How would your description and self talk change if you refocused your identity around your purpose?

4. How can you bring hope and encouragement into the world around you? What is one tangible step you can take in the near future to bring good news to those who need it?

chapter seven

PUTTING DOWN ROOTS

"BUT BLESSED ARE THOSE WHO TRUST IN THE LORD AND HAVE MADE THE LORD THEIR HOPE AND CONFIDENCE. THEY ARE LIKE TREES PLANTED ALONG A RIVERBANK, WITH ROOTS THAT REACH DEEP INTO THE WATER. SUCH TREES ARE NOT BOTHERED BY THE HEAT OR WORRIED BY LONG MONTHS OF DROUGHT. THEIR LEAVES STAY GREEN, AND THEY NEVER STOP PRODUCING FRUIT."
JEREMIAH 17:7-8 (NLT)

THE ANCHOR & THE LINE

I found good news! I found light in the darkness and hope where there had been none. No matter what came before or what might come next, every day would hold opportunities and potential for me to live in my purpose. No one chooses my value for me; no one else decides my future. I am not looking to avoid pain because I know that I cannot control what might or might not happen. And I know that my pain doesn't define me. This changes my perspective on the seasons of life and the limitless potential we all hold inside of us. If our circumstances do not determine our value, then that means we can pursue our goals and ambitions without fear! There is a HUGE difference between striving for more because you want to unlock your potential versus doing things because you need to in order to feel valuable.

I heard a pastor use this analogy once, and it stuck with me. When you go fishing, there is a critical difference between the anchor line and the fishing line. These are both lines that go off of your boat and into the water, but they have vastly different functions and roles. The anchor is a foundational connection, the primary root, that secures you to the ground. Tides will come in and out, waves and winds can beat against your boat, and the anchor will keep you grounded. A boat with no anchor may be fine for a time, but only in still and quiet waters. We've already covered my conviction that no one goes through every season of life on still and quiet waters; we all have storms and pains and struggles. A boat with no anchor will drift, crash into other boats, and lose its way. The anchor line is our most defining and inherent identity; it is our good news. So, for me, I finally found my anchor when I realized that I was known and loved by God no matter what I did or what had happened to me. From then until now, my anchor has only grown bigger and stronger and more secure. This is the most important and influential root that tethers me to my purpose and potential.

With my anchor line in place, I feel more freedom and joy to put fishing lines into the water. These lines represent my potential, my goals, and the things I'm striving for. I can fish for more in life because I want to, not because I have to. I can work and prepare and practice as much as I can to catch the big fish. I can set out multiple lines for my business, hobbies, fitness, and networking—all of these are opportunities to pursue excellence and strive to be my very best. However, no matter how good I get at casting, none of those fishing lines will serve as an anchor. Writing this book is a great example. I am putting a line out into life with hopes and ambitions to impact someone's life by telling my story in this book. There has been a lot of time and energy, and excellence put in so this book can be its best and reach its limitless potential. But if for any reason, this book doesn't get picked up, my life will go on because I'm not anchored in my opportunities.

At some point, everyone has made the error of mistaking their fishing line for their anchor. Literally? No, because being on a boat, there is no way you could mistake the two lines for each other. Metaphorically? Yes, we do this more often than we care to admit. We look at opportunities to make more money and hold on to that line as if our life depends on it. That line will not anchor you! It is a great line that can help you unleash your potential and strive to do your best, but it is not the line that is meant to hold you. Some relationships become false anchors, some titles are mistaken for core identities.

When we depend on fishing lines to be our anchors, we, and the people around us, can get hurt. The very worst scenarios are the stories we see in the news of a person, most often a man, who loses their job and returns home or comes back to the office to commit terrible acts of violence. This is the very worst case of someone who had failed to see the God-given anchor inside of them and acted as if their source of income or job title was their ultimate value or identity. Losing a job hurts like hell; spoiler alert, I've been there several times! If I never embraced the good news I'd found, I would have been tempted to lean on the wrong line and inevitably hurt myself or someone around me. It is important to see and know the difference between the anchor and the lines we cast out. Reach for the best and grow in everything we do. Not because we have to, but because we get to. Living in this mindset allows us to express our purpose and unleash our potential while maintaining a healthy perspective on our identity and self-worth. As my story continues, I would need to keep this mindset present at all times. Unfortunately, the devil is still outside doing push-ups, making waves, and trying to rock the boat.

STRONGER, NOT EASIER

I was living and working in Lexington, Kentucky. My love for movement and health grew; I was getting stronger and stronger: physically, emotionally, and mentally. Internally, my roots were growing and branching out, but life on the outside was still full of questions and pain. I was now in my mid-twenties, out of college and casting lines out looking for some bites. I had a job and was independent enough to be doing my own thing in Kentucky. One day, I'm heading off in my car to pick up some supplies for work when things go dark, and I mean lights out dark. The next thing I know, I'm being seen by a doctor in the hospital. The police report says that my car spun out of control, hit a light pole, and then went airborne into another vehicle. I was found hanging out of the passenger window, my seat belt torn, covered in blood. I was being told that I had a fracture in my neck, a brain hemorrhage, and would need staples in my head. My dad flew down from Illinois to help take care of me. It would take one more trip to the hospital to treat some swelling in my brain (it felt like my head was going to pop) and then three months for a full recovery for my neck and concussion.

My accident did not stop me from being outside and being active. Two years later, I would be out snowboarding, which I absolutely love, when disaster would strike again. I was doing tricks down a hill when I wiped out and broke my arm. My entire left arm and side hurt and I couldn't move them, but I didn't feel anything in my neck. I planned on just heading home, it was only about two hours away, but the resort required me to be seen and sent to the local hospital. It was the worst emergency room I've ever been to (and you can see I've been to a lot). It took hours for me to be seen. I got some various X-rays and MRIs, then they released me with a sling on my arm. The scans were forwarded to doctors at a University of Kentucky hospital, and the next morning, I got a call from them around

7:00 am. They told me not to move, an ambulance was on its way. No one told me why or what was going on.

After a long hour at the hospital, I was finally told that I had two fractured vertebrae and that I was lucky to be walking. Are you kidding me?! And the medical team near the ski resort just sent me home in a sling! The reason I could hardly move my left side or arm was because of the fractures and nerve damage in my neck. They first told me that if I had bumped into something on my way home from the resort or accidentally banged my head at home, or even turned my neck the wrong way—my neck could have fully broken and I would be looking at lifelong damage or paralysis. The good news was that had not happened, and with about a year of treatment and rehab, I could rebuild my neck strength back and regain feeling back in my arm.

In these moments, I could no longer help or change what had happened to me. Moving forward, the choice was mine to either do the hard work in recovery or retreat into myself and avoid the pain. Physically, I was as weak as I'd ever been. But I now know and understood that no matter what happens next, my purpose and value were untouchable. This doesn't make me fatalistic, it's quite the opposite. Everything has potential and everything matters. I'm just not defined by the results. I put in the time and work to recover, to learn how to take care of myself and return my strength. You have the power to grow, heal, and return strength when circumstances tear us down. There can be joy in the journey and purpose through the pain. In this season, I was rooted and anchored in truth, but I hadn't figured out where my purpose was leading me yet. Around this same time, both of my parents were dealing with illnesses, and I was able to be present and helpful. So, I returned home to Illinois to help with some family needs while also exploring some new opportunities for my own life. I got the chance to be a news producer at KHQA and their television station. This job would change my life and future forever. My anchor and roots would grow in ways I never knew they could.

ROOTED IN LOVE

I'm honestly not sure that everything happens for a reason; I prefer the idea that there is purpose through everything and potential in everything. However, I do feel like something led me to this opportunity. I had been living in Kentucky for around ten years and had a good job that paid well. I was independent and physically removed from some of the baggage of my past. Now I'm back home, living in a town that I didn't really like, working a job that I wasn't sure how to do, earning quite a bit less money than I had before. I had to remind myself that my purpose and potential are not bound up in my circumstances, so I tried to get the most out of this season and not tell myself limiting stories. I mean, I had some experience doing college station news and theatre. I can do this! Time to grow!

I right away noticed one co-worker, a reporter, and a weekend anchor. She was absolutely gorgeous! In the office, on set, it didn't matter—my attention kept wandering back towards her. I'd think,

"Wow, she is beautiful… how am I going to get her to notice me?" I was working hard, and it was paying off. In 2008, there was a major flood along the Mississippi River, and it was making national news because of the size and impact of the flooding waters. The scope of this news opened up some new opportunities in our station. I took this opportunity to be on camera and report the flood. This opportunity sparked more, and soon I was working to become a weekend weather anchor. Why not, right? I can try to work from behind and in front of the camera. I can put my face on television and talk. At one point in my life, I was being given special treatment for being a child who wouldn't talk or interact with anyone. Why can't I grow to become a television producer and weather anchor? Why couldn't I speak to that beautiful, intelligent, talented woman?

I started hanging out with my colleagues after work, and she would be there. One thing led to another, and our relationship took off! I found myself thriving in a place that I could have easily given up on. More than growing in my career, my heart was growing with the hope that I could be loved and be in love with someone. I had been in relationships before, but some of them burned down, and some just didn't go the distance. To be completely honest, I self-sabotaged some relationships due to some hidden fears and scars. There were some relationships that broke because I pursued women that were never going to treat me well; I knew that they would hurt me, but I wouldn't acknowledge it. Once I saw her, I couldn't think of anyone else. This woman was truly incredible, and I allowed myself to pursue our relationship to its limitless potential.

We dated for a couple of years, and one day we received the life-changing news that we were pregnant. This was an exciting and emotional time that, of course, came with some professional and personal stress. There were also layers of complexity from some people around us because I am a white man, and I was in a relationship with a black woman. It is the handiwork of the devil to press the iniquities from one generation on to the next. Some people, mostly from older generations, held on to corrupted and broken ideas of supremacy and racism. Some people, mostly "religious," held on to the idea that becoming pregnant before marriage was inexcusable and encouraged a quick elopement to save reputations. The iniquities of others, like cycles of pain, are often projected from one person to another.

We were in love! Neither of us was perfect, and life certainly allows for unplanned things to happen. The option before us was to live in the hate or guilt that other people were projecting onto us, or live in the secure identity and love that we had inside of us. Iniquities and cycles of pain are tools that the devil uses to build walls between people. He loves to limit us from connecting and uniting with others. Faith and truth in our God-given identity can be limited by the expectations and graceless application of "religious" people. When God clearly aims to forgive and love, some people are driven to withhold mercy or compassion. We decided to reject the hate and guilt and remain fixed, rooted in love.

Our daughter would be born in the coming months and my life and roots were growing. When you build a family, the root of love and faith in yourself grows to hold the love you have for your partner and your children. I am now stronger for having this beautiful and strong woman in my life. And I am now stronger for having this sweet little baby girl in my arms. They are attached to my core. We did not rush into marriage because we wanted to make it our decision and no one else's. But now we were ready to officially intertwine our hearts and lives forever, or at least I would officially make that proposal. So, one day at work, I was on live television giving a weather update as my gorgeous partner was sitting at her anchor desk. The broadcast was going out to homes all across our region as I turned to Alexis and got down on one knee. You can go and watch the video on YouTube, it has over 2.5 million views! She said yes, and we would be off into the next new chapter of our life together.

IN SICKNESS AND IN HEALTH

Did I mention that life is good? Have I also mentioned that pain sneaks in when we are least expecting it? Our wedding was quickly approaching, and we were so excited. I was feeling good, feeling blessed. I felt that way because it was true! The reality that life can be painful does not diminish the moments when things are easy or comfortable. We should never cry when the sun is going down; we should soak in the view and appreciate the beauty of what is happening around us. When things are at their darkest, we remind ourselves that the sun will come up again, and ease and comfort will return eventually. Most of all, we can hold on to hope, and peace, and joy through all of it. We have purpose through the pain.

So, obviously, I'm setting something up. Let's get into it. My life and work are closely connected to my physical health and strength. I am at the gym all of the time, and before I owned and operated my own gym, I would attend a local gym to maintain my body. I believe that I got something from the gym I was going to. One day I began having this terrible headache, I mean horrible pain between my ears. It lasted for two days, so I finally went to an urgent care center. They dismissed it as a migraine, but I knew that couldn't be right. After two more days, I found myself waking up in the middle of the night with a skull-splitting pain in my head. It was like there were claws breaking through my skull from the inside, trying to get out. As a man who has experienced a lot of pain, I believe this was the worst physical pain I've experienced. I thought I was going to die!

The hospital threw everything they had at me. Relief slowly came from treatments, but they had a hard time determining what was going on with me. Finally, the diagnosis came in, and apparently, I had some very rare form of meningitis. They told me that they were sending my test results off to different states to be studied at various labs and institutions. How about that as a badge of honor? Recovery finally came, and a week later, we had our wedding. It was a wonderful moment, as weddings typically are. I do reflect on our vows and the vows I hear today when we go to celebrate others at their weddings. We make these promises and commitments to each other, proclaiming that no matter what life throws at us—we will get through it together. A wedding vow is the essence of holding on to purpose through pain, to being rooted in love so that nothing could tear us down. It is a beautiful day but what is really incredible about weddings is how often we forget the power of our vows. Words matter. If we say something and mean it, we begin our journey in the confidence that we will push through it for richer or poorer, in sickness and in health. I'm glad my wife could look at me, knowing how much of a magnet I seem to be for pain, and still vow to stand by me through it all. I will never be perfect, and neither will she, but we didn't commit to perfection—we committed to each other.

Thank God because I gave my wife many more opportunities to live out her vows. About one month after we got married, I began having the worst gut issues. At first, I thought it was just gas, but it kept getting worse, and I just knew it was something else. Something felt wrong. So, I once again rushed to the hospital. I quickly found out that my appendix was about to burst! The doctors ended up removing it, which led to conditions and complications that I still live with today. This moment would change the way that I eat forever. As a health and fitness guru, I understand what I'm saying and asking when I tell a client that they need to change their dietary habits. I know how difficult that can be. But easy things are rarely helpful, and each of us is more capable than we realize.

THE RETURN

Between these two recent trips to the hospital, I brought home tens of thousands of dollars in medical debt. Our family was on EBT (Electronic Benefit Transfer) and food stamps. Money was tight, to say it kindly. Then, I nearly had my vehicle repossessed. At this point, I'm just rounding out my experiences with pain and struggle. I want you to know that I am sharing these moments and stories to build a case for what I believe to be true about you and about me: we can find purpose through pain. No matter what circumstances and seasons of life we walk through, our values and potential cannot be taken away from us. We adjust and pivot, we grow more patient and resolved. We honor the commitments we've made to our loved ones, and we never give up because, in the end, we know that we will win.

The truth is, there are so many more details and painful moments that I could have shared with you but decided not to. Perhaps we can talk about my other scars one on one or in another book. For now, I just hope you take some encouragement and some pause from what I've shared from my life so far. Whatever it is that you have been through or are going through, you are not alone in your pain. If you are like me, and you are the victim of abuse, you are not alone, and there is hope for you. If you have ever wondered, "does it get better, or is the pain all there is?" I can promise you that it does get better, and your value and life were never as lost as they felt.

Through all of the pain, I knew that my purpose was to bring light into the world. I was rooted in love, and nothing could overpower the strength that I held inside. My life holds more potential than I realized, so I can tell a bigger and better story than anyone can see right now. Through this season of life and debt, we continued to practice what we preached, and we found joy and strength to move forward. Our son was born, and our roots grew stronger. Then our third child, a daughter, was born, and our roots grew stronger still. Our faith grew stronger, and our love grew stronger. Piece by piece, moment by moment, we all grew together. I found clarity in my direction and launched my own business and career in health and fitness. I love my family, and I love what I get to do every day!

People tell me that I appear to be the most energetic and optimistic person they have ever met, and they might be right. I know that they see me today and they assume that 1) their pain is too much for them to move forward and grow, and 2) it must have been easy for me to get to where I am now. By this point, I hope you know that neither of those thoughts is true. Our pain is never too much to allow us to move forward, and I am still challenged each day by the devil outside doing push-ups. In fact, I've had a figure from my past reappear in my life in these past years, causing more trouble and forcing me to confront my pain. I still support my family, which includes the family member who abused me all of those years ago. He still has his scars from the babysitter as I do, but we have responded to pain with different choices throughout life. There was an opportunity for him and me to reconnect as a family, and I had to decide how I would handle this moment.

It is no small thing to confront your pain or your past. It isn't something you need to do alone, there are so many sources of support, and I recommend seeking them out. As for my story, I made the decision to forgive and allow some measured reconciliation to take place. I felt like that was the right decision to make, it was a way for me to move forward, and perhaps it would spark some more light and growth in that family. The reality is, we are not defined by our external circumstances, and we cannot control what the people around us do. After a short time of peace, this family member lost control of himself and made efforts to sabotage my business and threaten my family. Now I had no choice but to move forward by not allowing this person near my family. I share this story because it is important to know that we are not responsible for the choices that other people make, but we are responsible for our own decisions.

I also want you to understand that there are times when we do the right thing, but we don't get the result that we want. I was in a place to offer reconciliation, but the other party ultimately declined. No one needs to remain in a situation or relationship that continues to cause pain and destruction in their life. Growing through pain doesn't mean that you sit in front of a pitching machine and let it continue to hit you with fastballs. When you know your worth and purpose, then you can have the grace to forgive and potentially reconcile. However, we do not owe it to anyone to remain in a relationship or situation that continues to degrade our value or attempt to rob us of our potential. Do not return to old sources of pain or allow yourself to be stuck with them. If a past source of pain wants to return to your life, then it cannot return as a source of pain. Reconciliation is a two-way street; you and that old source can only reconnect if you are both changed, and you both have the heart to no longer give or receive pain. You are growing and changing as you unlock the limitless potential inside of you, but you cannot make anyone else grow or change. You have a strength and a purpose that no one can take from you. Do not let anyone or anything tell you otherwise.

TAKEAWAYS & GROWTH QUESTIONS

This is a chapter that wraps up my story for now. In the coming chapters, we will highlight the foundations of this book, and we will cover our four quadrants of success. I will include a few more stories and adventures in those chapters, but I want you to remember that my life isn't over yet! As long as you and I have breath, then we have purpose and love. No one can rob us of our value when we are rooted in love. I am blessed to have my wife and my three children; they have become part of my core, my very strongest root. In this chapter, I got to walk through more of life's pain and struggle, but I was never walking alone. Here are the key takeaways for this chapter:

1. We are anchored by the truth of what is inside of us; the root of our identity does not come from outside of ourselves. We shouldn't mistake our ambitions, successes, or failures as our identity.

2. There is no guarantee that life will be perfect. However, we can get stronger and discover more joy along the way.

3. We must be committed to the purpose we hold inside of ourselves. Like a wedding vow, we are resolute in our identity and promise to get through anything. The circumstances of life can change our methods and practices, but they never change our mission.

Take some time to go through these growth questions. As always, you have several options for how you can work your way through them. Be honest with yourself and the people you may be sharing your thoughts with. The choice is always yours; choose to be authentic. If you have your own questions, then add them to your reflection and discussion! Here are the questions I'm offering for this chapter:

1. What are your thoughts on the "anchor and the line" analogy? Do you ever look for self-worth or security in your ambitions or success? How can you be more resilient in life when the currents change?

2. How have you gotten stronger as you have moved through life? How have you learned to grow through the different seasons of your life?

3. Where is love in your life right now? What connection does love have with your roots or purpose?

4. What commitments do you have that you will keep, no matter what?

5. Have you ever been in a position to reconcile with someone who has hurt you in the past? How did your experience go?

chapter eight

PURPOSE THROUGH PAIN

"WE PUSH THROUGH THE ADVERSITY
AND PAIN, REMAIN ROOTED IN OUR
PURPOSE, AND PURSUE LIMITLESS POTENTIAL
DESPITE THE OBSTACLES AROUND US."
JUSTEN ARNOLD

IN DEFIANCE OF GRAVITY

For the first time in my life, the devil outside doing push-ups was afraid of me. He could never hit me hard enough to where I didn't get back up. He will always be out there, he will always puff out his chest and talk trash, but he knows that I know the truth. Just as consistent as the devil, life on Earth has constant oppositions and forces of nature. The easiest to identify is gravity. There is no human being who can jump from the ground and float off into space. No one can flap their arms and soar off into the sunset. Gravity is a real and constant force that pushes us down to Earth, keeps our dreams grounded. The opposition of gravity impacts everyone.

Human history has been flightless for thousands of years! Gravity is an abundant force, and the story that we told ourselves was that we could not overcome it. Mankind could only dream of joining the birds in the air or the stars in the night sky; the reality of gravity was too heavy to see our dreams come true or turn our hope into reality. Over the centuries, the dream of flight remained repressed while gravity earned the notoriety of scientific method, scientific law, and scientific theory. Gravity seemed to grow heavier as it became more understood and accepted as a universal force in our world. The pain of gravity is real; ask anyone who has fallen off their chair, slipped down the steps, or got pooped on by a bird. How ignorant it would be to imagine that we would ever touch the sky.

Thankfully, there were people who were beyond ignorant, they were daring and determined and limitless. These individuals dared to believe in something greater than the circumstances around them, to believe that no matter how many times the apple fell from the tree, human flight was possible. These individuals found limitless potential through the pain and presence of gravity. Plans were made, and plans failed, yet the purpose remained. Then came the day when two brothers soared for 12 long seconds. The very laws of nature that appeared to be immovable objects actually provided stability and control for sustained flight. Soon planes were flying across state lines, national borders, and oceans. The purpose of flight and exploration launched us through and beyond gravity, to the moon and back again. If you tried to explain to someone 1,000 years ago that one day we would put a bunch of men, women, and children into a metal tube with wings and fly thousands of miles above the ground—their heads would explode!

We dared to defy gravity, and we conquered the skies. What was once an impossible dream is now a common practice and routine part of life. Beyond flight, we are now less afraid to fall. People jump out of airplanes and off of tall buildings and safely parachute down to the ground. The wildest thing I've ever seen are videos of the people base jumping while wearing wingsuits; these flying squirrel-like suits allow them to glide as they free fall, you need to look it up and watch if you haven't seen it before. Again, humanity has taken what was once an obstacle and turned it into a playground. We fly, and we fall despite gravity. And when we fail, we get back up and try again.

This is just like the good news that I discovered, which, again, will change your life if you accept it. Our potential and purpose are stronger than our external circumstances and oppositions. For centuries, the constant obstacle and opposition of gravity crushed our dreams of flight and limited our potential for travel and exploration. If our potential and purpose were established only by what was happening around us, then we would still be looking up to the sky, waiting for gravity to change or disappear. Instead, we allowed our purpose and potential to move through and grow beyond our perceived limitations. Despite the constant pull of gravity, we now get to pack our bags and fly to a tropical destination or see the wonders of the world around us.

This is what it means to be limitless. This is the root of belief and assurance that breaks through the rocks and grows beyond the obstacles. Because of gravity, we could not float above the ground or flap our arms and fly away. The dream and purpose of flight have clearly been inside of human hearts and minds, it just didn't seem possible for a very long time. This is the perfect example of finding purpose in pain and unleashing limitless potential. In this life, we will find struggles and pain, but we can push through and grow despite them. We will often be tempted to wait for circumstances to change, but the power is in us to rise above perceived limitations. Do not let your story be told merely by what is happening around you. Take the purpose inside of you and unleash your limitless potential by telling a bigger and better story through your life.

PURPOSE

I want to remind you that you are not to blame yourself for the circumstances or decisions that exist around you. No one deserves to be hurt, and you certainly did not ask to go through the difficult moments that life tossed at you. The world we live in is broken, there are cracks in the foundation and they all run deep. Each of us suffers the pain of a broken world, and too often, we ignore it and hide it. The healing answer to pain is purpose. To be our truest self is to fly in defiance of gravity. Every pain is an attempt to push us down, block our growth, and grind us into dust. There is a way through the pain that doesn't break us down or belittle our values. There is a path for us to take, and there is no better time than now to grow.

The road forward is unique for each of us, and I cannot prescribe a one size fits all approach to handling pain. However, this book includes the pieces of my journey of purpose in response to the pain of my life. When pain comes around, we need to connect to our purpose. I believe that God has given each of us purpose. You have a purpose! So often we mistake our career or favorite hobby with our purpose, but that isn't it. Michael Jordan is the greatest basketball player in the universe, but his purpose in life is not to put a ball in a hoop. Purpose runs deeper than that. My belief is firm that purpose is inside all of us. My purpose is to be a light and help others find joy and strength inside of them, to help others move better, feel better, and live better. How I do that can change, maybe I won't own and operate a gym forever, and that is fine because that isn't my purpose. Circumstances can change, pain can come in any form or fashion, but my strength and purpose remain. So, when pain knocks at the door, the first thing we need to do is find and hold our purpose. This is the first and most important step.

I know a lot of people struggle to identify or articulate their purpose; it is one of the most common questions asked, "Who am I and why am I here?" For some, defining purpose is hard to do. Sometimes we wonder if we are here for any reason other than to suffer. I promise you there is something deeper and more powerful than that feeling. I believe that everyone's purpose in life is connected to this passage in the Bible that invites us to be loved by God and to demonstrate love to others. There is a passage in 1 John 4 that says that we cannot look up into the sky and see God, but God's love is made visible when we show love to each other. To be known and loved is near the core of every person's purpose. You need to take some time to write out a purpose statement for your life. A phrase or sentence that you can rest on when circumstances change, when pain inevitability arises. Once you've got it, you'll see that nothing can take that truth away from you. If your purpose statement can change with a job loss, account balance change, or health scare—then you need to work on your purpose statement some more.

Your purpose will shine through any darkness, any pain. It doesn't always lessen the pain, but it makes you stronger and more capable of moving forward through anything. Purpose doesn't make you invincible, it makes you eternal. Find joy in the journey of discovering who you really are and how God has wired you to make an impact on the world. No one can stand against what God has placed inside of you. Pain will come, and it might hurt like hell, but identity and purpose inside of us have the power to withstand anything that life can throw at us. Purpose will unlock your limitless potential because your life is not dependent on or defined by your external circumstances. Your purpose is the engine that allows you to fly despite the gravity around you. Hold tight to your purpose and look for the limitless potential all around you!

COMFORTABLE BEING UNCOMFORTABLE

We all experience pain and obstacles just like we all experience gravity. There is no avoiding it or wishing it away, it comes for us all and impacts us all in one form or another. The devil is outside doing push-ups, hoping to kick your ass if you let him. There are really three options for us in life:

1. We push through adversity and pain, remain rooted in our purpose, and pursue limitless potential despite the obstacles around us.
2. We wander aimlessly as the waves and winds of life bat us around, our circumstances drive our direction, and our situations define our value and meaning.
3. We avoid painful and challenging situations altogether, our dreams are isolated from reality, and growth and fulfillment become sacrifices on us to alter comfort and pleasure.

Every decision we make, every path we take, follows one of those three directions. The second and third options are the widest and most popular roads to travel. There is a temptation to believe that the first option is the scariest, the most painful, and perhaps the most humiliating path to take; confronting your pain, pushing through obstacles, and trying new things can appear to be daunting and uncomfortable. What if I fail? What if talking about my pain makes it worse? What will happen if I make that change in my life? This little voice whispers fearful concerns and invites you to either take path #2, where we just go through life with the status quo and hope things change on their own, or take path #3, where we stay inside our bubble and avoid pain or failure by never trying or venturing out into the world. This voice wants us to believe that staying in our house or living in the status quo is the most comfortable option.

- "Stay with what is familiar."
- "Hold on to old habits."
- "Never look in the mirror."

When it is spelled out in front of us, we can see that these are fearful thoughts and actions; you and I would likely agree that living in the status quo or hiding from the world are not the best routes for us to take. But we may be defaulting into those mindsets more often than we realize, especially in our mundane day-to-day moments. How many times have you talked yourself out of something because it was uncomfortable, or you are too tired? How often do you put something off until tomorrow? Very few people intentionally plan to coast through life or shelter in place, but we all are tempted to think that way when it comes to daily decisions and habits. When we sell out a dream for something convenient and comfortable, we are limiting potential and stifling our purpose. When we bottle up our feelings, avoid conflict, lie, hit the snooze button, skimp on our exercise, or break our diets—we are letting a momentary convenience or comfort rob us of a bigger goal or growth.

Those voices want us to believe that it is more comfortable and safer when we avoid failure and pain. However, this mentality ultimately results in more pain and more discomfort down the road. Back to gravity for a moment, some people live as if they need gravity to change in order for flight to be possible. Instead of working through the obstacle, they just wait for the obstacle to change or leave so that they do not have to do the hard work or growth needed to move through it. But if gravity did cease to exist, life and flight wouldn't be easier or more convenient, it would be horrifying and painful as we slowly drift out of our atmosphere and into the cold dark vacuum of space. A life with no obstacles is not comfortable or painless; waiting for circumstances to change outsources our purpose and potential to the randomness of the world we live in. Staying inside your house and hiding from pain and failure doesn't give you peace or freedom, it makes you a prisoner. The devil outside knows that you are stronger than him, so his greatest and most desperate moves are to convince you to either never fight back or stay locked up inside. Either way, he wins, and you lose! Easy comes with a price, and it is most often the cost of your purpose and potential.

In order to truly live life to the fullest, we must live out our purpose and unleash our limitless potential. To do this, we must become comfortable being uncomfortable. Pushing through the obstacles requires us to willingly and willfully step out into the world and deal with the shit that we see and feel. If we want to have limitless fitness, then we need to do the hard work and push through the pain of growing healthier and stronger. If we want to have a limitless family, then we need to fight for what is best and honor the commitments that we made. Some of us work so much and so hard because we are confusing a full life with a busy life. It takes work to slow down and let our purpose grow beyond our busyness. We may believe we will only be comfortable once we have "enough" money or the right job title, but that is a false identity and purpose. Sometimes we need to be more comfortable with the discomfort of not being a millionaire or CEO. Perhaps that money or that title is in our future, but neither will be our defining purpose or characteristic in life. Being rooted in our identity and self-worth requires us to be a little uncomfortable in the other areas of our life, and that needs to be alright. We will never have everything, but we can have everything we need. We will not live forever on this Earth, but we can leave a legacy that impacts those we leave behind.

Taking path #1 requires us to boldly move forward with our focus on the future. When we are confident in who we are and what we believe, we can work through any past or present circumstance. Be comfortable being uncomfortable. Face the pain. It will help you grow. Each pain that I experienced created a painful memory and a painful road to recovery. If I settled for momentary comfort or pleasure, then I would never have come out of car accidents and skiing accidents as a stronger and healthier person. I would have never found forgiveness for myself or for others. My story is a testament to confronting life and pain head-on, to finding joy and passion in the pursuit of living in our purpose. The journey of writing this book was like a series of forks in the road, daily choices between doing something easy and doing something worthy of my purpose. Purpose through pain requires consistent and intentional choices to do what is often hard and uncomfortable. Growth comes from outside of our comfort zone. You have more power and control in your life when you leave the safety net of the past and move forward into the future.

LEAN IN AND LIVE

What do we do with our pain? Everyone experiences struggles and storms, we all have trouble in our rearview mirror. So, what do we do with our pain as we move through it and grow beyond it? I believe we need to lean into our story and let our pain inspire us and fuel our purpose. That may sound counterproductive, definitely countercultural, but I promise this is a game-changer. Leaning into hard times has been transformative for me. When I left for college, I wanted to have a fresh start in life. I was tempted to ignore the pain of my past and go off into a world where no one would ever have to know what happened to me. But something inside of me knew that would be wrong, knew that would actually hold me back. So, I joined a campus group that encouraged and educated other students dealing with abuse. I started sharing my story of sexual abuse, broken bones, rare diseases, struggles with gut health, and all of the other forms of pain that I've encountered. By leaning into my story and my pain, I found that I could make a positive impact on others. I found that I was growing in ways that I wasn't sure were possible. Instead of hiding from pain, I leaned in, and now I am writing a book. My pain doesn't hold me back, it inspires me to help others and grow in my purpose and potential. There are opportunities in our pain. It's not that we are thankful for the hurt and the pain, but that it can be a vehicle of sorts towards our purpose that not only transforms our lives but the lives we come in contact with.

As new pain enters my life, leaning in allows me to see it with a different perspective. I recently had a procedure, and the doctor found some pre-cancerous polyps. There are all of the normal and healthy emotions of concern and care for my health and future. Leaning into the pain of this moment meant that I could pause to find purpose through this moment. I could see the silver linings that would become shining lights in this season. They found the polyps and removed them before anything could grow or develop to be more dangerous or harmful. Leaning in puts me in control of my emotional and mental state as I navigate through obstacles. When I'm at the gym, I can lean into the pain of my muscles because I know that this process is building me up to be stronger. This changes my outlook on pain and failure, and it puts me in the driver's seat as I navigate life and discover new potential in every season. Do not be afraid of failure. Lean in and learn from your experiences. Every failure holds opportunities for growth.

Some people let pain or failure stop them from moving forward, and that is a tragedy. You have the choice to live or die. Some people die at 25 years old but aren't buried until they turn 85 years old. Something happened in their twenties that made them quit, take their foot off the gas, and stop living. They go on to exist for decades longer, but that is all they are doing—existing. Life is more than breath. When we stop challenging ourselves, we stop learning, which means we stop moving forward, which means we stop living. Lean into life and make it count. Do not wait for life to be perfect or painless. Life isn't about waiting for the storms to pass. It is about dancing in the rain—which I love to do. Lean in where you are, explore your life, and scrap every piece of joy and adventure out of it. Do not let life knock you down. If you do get knocked down, then get back up and lean in. Embrace the truth that every season of life holds something good for you because there is good inside of you. You have a purpose inside of you!

A NEW STANDARD

I love talking with people in my gym, at my church, at the barbershop, hiking in the woods… honestly, I love talking with people everywhere I go. Through my own life's growth and development, I've learned a lot about unleashing my potential in my finances, family, fitness, and faith. So, I naturally talk about these subjects and the most recent books or studies that I've come across regarding growth and potential. When we get into daily habits and personal goals, I honestly have found that most people agree with what I wrote in the last section: that we need to lean into the pain and do the hard work required to grow. Again, this is a principle that most people will nod their heads to and give their stamp their approval; I rarely hear someone say, "I'm too lazy to build healthier habits" or "I'm too comfortable with the status quo." However, what I hear so often is "I just don't have time to do all of that," "I wish I could fit that into my budget," or "well, I used to be like you, but I don't have enough energy now."

Have you ever said those words out loud? Have you ever told yourself one of those excuses when the opportunity for limitless potential presented itself? We all have fallen into this trap at some point in our lives. It is time to snap out of it!

Set your life around your standards, not your standards around your life. Our standards, values, and practices do not have to be limited by circumstances. Let's use an example as our schedule. I've been told over and over that someone just doesn't have enough time to do something that brings life and purpose to their day. The assumption is that their life determines their schedule, which means that they are giving away control of their time to whatever forces are surrounding them. Today life may give me time for passion and purpose, but tomorrow it may not. When the storms of life rage against us, we can often end up tossing important things overboard, believing that they will prevent us from sinking. Living this way means our standards, commitments, and habits are always conditional. They are at the will and mercy of the chaos around us. Life happens so fast. If you wait until life gets easier or more comfortable, then you will likely never grow to have healthy standards. Time will fly by, and you will have missed countless opportunities because you were allowing your standards and habits to be dictated by the world around you.

Do not readjust your standards as the wind blows. Set the standards in stone and adjust your life around them. This means our true priorities and passions and purpose find a place in our schedule because we set our own standard for our time. If we are honest with ourselves, we waste a lot more time each day than we realize. Decide what daily practices and habits you want to see to shape in your life, and then plan out your day around them. You will be shocked to see how much time you can regain when you wake up on time, cut out excessive social media use, take advantage of time commuting to work, and plan out your entire day. In each of the next four chapters, we will have some examples of how you can set a new standard for yourself in the four quadrants of success. Do not settle for less by letting the chaos and pain of life be in control. Set your standards for who you want to be and how you want to live, and then make plans and do the hard work of setting those plans in motion. You will be blessed when you take ownership of your life. And you will be a greater blessing to those around you when your best self is growing and thriving for all to enjoy.

TAKEAWAYS & GROWTH QUESTIONS

While it can be hard to imagine, there can be a design for your suffering. You truly can have immense impact and potential because of it, not despite it. It is time to move forward and grow. This chapter holds some foundational elements that we will explore more in the final four chapters. We will explore purpose, leaning in, and setting standards in four key areas: fitness, finances, family, and faith. Here are the key takeaways for this chapter:

1. You have a purpose that is greater than the circumstances of your life. When we face moments of pain and seasons of struggle, we need to find identity and strength in our purpose because it will never change or be taken from us.

2. Lean into your pain, do not run away from it. Leaning in allows us to see growth and opportunities in every situation, no matter how hard. Our pain can be a fuel and inspiration that pushes us to new heights and new hope as we use our experiences to impact the world around us.

3. Set your life around your standards, not your standards around your life. Our standards, values, and practices do not have to be limited by circumstances. Take control over your life and establish the rhythms through your purpose.

Take some time to go through these growth questions. As always, you have several options for how you can work your way through them. Be honest with yourself and the people you may be sharing your thoughts with. The choice is always yours; choose to be authentic. If you have your own questions, then add them to your reflection and discussion! Here are the questions I'm offering for this chapter:

1. Gravity is a constant struggle and force against flight, but inspired people saw limitless potential in the presence of adversity and pushed through the obstacle. What oppositions and adversities are in your life right now?

2. What is your purpose statement? How would you give definition and words to your heart's ambition and mission?

3. What is the difference between failure and giving up? Are there areas in your life where you give up too easily?

4. What have you learned from failure in your life so far? How did it impact you or inspire you to succeed in the future?

5. What are you doing in your life right now that is difficult and sometimes uncomfortable so that you will grow and move forward towards your dreams?

6. What standards do you hold for your everyday life? What principles and passions do you want to win in the competition between your schedule, budget, and energy? How can you adjust your habits and priorities to establish the right priorities in your life?

chapter nine

LIMITLESS FITNESS

"YOU CANNOT CONTROL WHAT HAPPENS
IN THE WORLD AROUND YOU, BUT YOU CAN
CONTROL YOURSELF. TELL A BETTER STORY,
LIVE A BETTER AND MORE FULFILLING LIFE,
AND UNLEASH YOUR LIMITLESS POTENTIAL."
JUSTEN ARNOLD

A NEW PERSPECTIVE ON FITNESS & HEALTH

Have you ever flexed your muscles so hard that your clothes began to rip? Have you ever lifted so much weight that the ground began to crack beneath your feet? Have you ever tried opening a door only to crush the doorknob in your hand? You haven't? Good, because neither have I. Let's talk about limitless fitness. The health and fitness industry is amazing, and I love being a leader and coach in this space. One thing that I encounter in clients and other fitness leaders is the idea that fitness and health are exclusively tied to strength, muscle mass, and extremely low body fat. You may not realize it, but this thought often comes from the subliminal cues we pick up at the grocery store (the magazines in the check-out line), watching various forms of entertainment (movies and television stars with similar body types), and social media (flooded with influencers and edited photos to make arms look bigger and waistlines look smaller). The subconscious thought is often a comparison: if that is what it looks like to be fit and healthy, then I've got no chance!

Comparison is a thief of joy, but it is also a thief of potential. There are billions of people on this planet! This idea that fitness and health come in one shape and size is outrageous and harmful to the uniqueness of every person.

We are going to take this all the way back to our first chapter— the illustration of climbing a mountain and enjoying the journey along the way. Life, fitness, and health are each like a never-ending mountain that we get to navigate and climb up. Too often, we limit ourselves and our potential by comparing our current place on the mountain and our path forward with someone else's. We see someone who appears more fit than we are, and we see the path that they took towards growth, so we assume that is the place we need to be, and their path towards growth is the only way forward. "If only I could get to where they are; if only I could do what they do and eat as little as they must eat." If we aren't careful, our motivation for growing and climbing higher in life, fitness, and health is warped into self-loathing and self-hate for where we are and who we are, especially in comparison to someone else.

We need a new perspective on fitness and health, and it starts with shifting your focus away from everyone else and finding joy in your own journey. No one starts in the same place. No one has the same path forward. Where are you now in your fitness and health? Where do you want to go? How do you want to get there? This is your body, your life, your journey. You can't trade in your body for someone else's, so don't bother comparing or self-loathing; embrace your growth and climb the mountain with satisfaction. Being fit and healthy is a lifelong journey. You haven't arrived yet, and neither has anyone else. Your perspective needs to focus on how you will grow from this season on through the next, what you are going to learn and explore on your way, and how you can find joy in your movement. More than anything, the perspective we have on fitness and health goes deeper than the "where, what, and how" questions. Our journey up the mountain has to be rooted in our answer to "why?" Trust me, I don't see anyone make long-term and healthy progress in their fitness and health without a good reason. Self-hate can get some people in the gym. They hate the way they look, they hate the way they feel, they hate that they don't look like someone else… but that never develops into a real strong reason to grow. Hate is a terrible motivator, and it quickly turns from a reason to grow into a reason to self-destruct. You need to tell a better story, one that honors the purpose and potential inside of you.

THE STORY WE TELL OURSELVES: FITNESS & HEALTH

It really all comes back, full circle, to these principles from the first chapter. The story we tell ourselves is either the most helpful tool or it is a limiting weight that we carry with us. When it comes to fitness and health, what stories have you told yourself in the past? What story are you telling today? Do you feel like you are moving closer to your fitness and health potential, or are you moving farther away from it? We cannot control the circumstances around us or the things that happen to us. We cannot change gravity, and we cannot expect a painless existence. However, we do have control over our next steps forward as we respond with either creativity or destruction. The way we believe, think, and talk about our fitness and health journey matters. One of the biggest weights and obstacles that I find holding people back is the story that they are telling themselves.

- "No one in my family is fit. We aren't built like that."
- "I don't feel comfortable at the gym, and running is the worst."
- "I'm too old and past my prime. When I was younger, it was easier to stay in shape."
- "I always quit, so what's the point in trying again?"

No one can unlock the limitless potential inside of them while they are telling self-defeating and limiting stories about themselves. Those negative and critical stories that we tell are not only excuses for not trying or quitting in the future. They are truly old wounds acting up from our past. We may say some things as a joke, but it is often a painful experience from the past that is manifesting itself now as an excuse not to grow. Whether we were hurt by our own failure or someone else's, we need to push through the pain and discover some new optimism for our future. If our story remains negative and destructive, then we will miss out on our potential. More often than not, the story we tell ourselves will become our reality. These are self-fulfilling prophecies that we manifest into outcomes. If the story I tell is that I'll never do something, then guess what? I'll never do it! Negativity and destruction are a vicious cycle: we fail, we believe we are not capable of success or worth the effort, and so we fail again and again until we quit. We all fail. It is part of life. We need to forgive ourselves and hold on to a more optimistic outcome for our future.

The story we tell ourselves needs to be rooted in self-love and belief. You can learn from your past and do better next time. You can get back into your fitness and health routines and stay committed to them. You are worth building up and growing to unleash your potential. The world needs it. You are going to feel better and better as you grow and climb the mountain. There are ways to achieve your fitness and health goals that you will enjoy and find satisfaction in. You are becoming the best version of yourself, one day at a time, gaining strength of heart and mind as well as strength in your body. You are going to feel better than you previously thought you could because you deserve to be and feel your best. You will never be perfect, but you can always give yourself a fresh start and try again. You can get stronger, move better, and improve your physical capacity. You cannot control what happens in the world around you, but you can control yourself. Tell a better story, live a better and more fulfilling life, and unleash your limitless potential.

BE POSITIVE & BE INTENTIONAL

There is another layer to positivity and self-love that I want to touch on for a moment. The story you tell is the first step in unleashing your fitness and health potential. As you begin to take action and build new habits, you will need to establish positive and intentional moments in your day. Think of it this way, we all understand that you need to stay hydrated, especially when you are working on your fitness and health. Building positive and intentional moments in your day is like refreshing your heart, mind, and body with a cool glass of water. It can be hard to tell a better story when you are tired, depleted, and dry. Be positive and be intentional in your day-to-day life, and you will find it easier to remain optimistic and energized to grow and climb through the seasons of your life. Being positive means adding moments into your day that will inspire and fuel the life, purpose, and potential that you hold—being intentional means using your effort, energy, and schedule to make growth and self-love purposeful and make it a priority.

One of my favorite daily habits that are positive and intentional are my brief moments of meditation. I would never have imagined that a guy like me with ADHD would structure mediation into his daily routine. These moments typically last for one to five minutes, and I use this tool a couple of times each day. I take a quiet moment, often driving in the car or getting ready in the morning, and I take some slow, deep breaths. I often breathe deeply six times, and I say, "I am a son of God, I have everything that I need" with each exhale. This practice fills me up with courage and strength, and it encourages me to believe greater things about myself and what I'm capable of.

Again, positivity makes all the difference. The devil is outside doing push-ups. He will use anything he can to knock you down and put his foot on your back. Finding and embracing a positive mindset is key to unlocking the growth and strength you need to stay on your feet and move forward. Being positive and intentional not only fuels your heart and mind, but there are also studies that show that these sources of encouragement and confidence actually cause a physical change in your body. I came across a study on hotel employees across multiple locations. They divided the employees across all locations into two groups. Group A was told that their daily work at the hotel was an incredible exercise and was good for their health. The other half, Group B, did not say anything at all. Both groups continued to do their normal jobs for about a month. They tested and reviewed the health of all employees at the end of that time and found that Group A had lower weight, lower blood pressure, lower body fat, and several other fitness and health indicators. Simply believing that their regular daily work makes a positive impact seemed to actually inspire a tangible positive impact in their fitness and health.

Another study showed that people who imagined flexing their biceps five times a week for 12 weeks showed a 13.5% increase in muscle strength. Other studies have shown that our posture and facial expression impact our mood and emotions. We all know that it works the other way around: a bad mood often inspires us to walk around like Charlie Brown with our head and shoulders slumped down. However, there are scientific indications that show that good posture and positive facial expressions actually lift our spirit and emotions. We can actually feel better by being intentional with the way we sit and by building moments when we can smile and laugh with someone else. Don't just move around aimlessly, and don't allow yourself to be stuck in a funk about your life, fitness, and health. Avoid using shame or punishment as fuel for exercise; waiting until you feel bad enough to move is a miserable way to live and will not provide you with consistent or helpful motivation to move. Exercise is a celebration of what your body can do. It is not punishment. Be positive and be intentional. It makes a huge difference.

MOVEMENT IS KING

Everyone wants to look good; others want to look like someone else. Either way, there is a gap between where we are and where we want to be. That is a good thing; it means we have breath in our lungs, and we have more room to grow and climb higher in life.

The problem is that so many times, we find the path forward to be boring, annoying, or just plain miserable. This reality has shaped my approach to coaching and gym management. I could teach you all of the various lifting methods, exercises, routines, and equipment used to break down fat and build muscle; I know all of it! However, I also know that you need to do every single one of those exercises, and it would be a struggle to find the motivation to do them at home or do them consistently for a long period of time.

If you came to my gym, we would focus on building a personal fitness plan more than parroting some random fitness routine. Each of us is drawn to different forms and types of movement, and movement is better than exercise. Think of it this way; exercise is often limited to a gym or to a treadmill, or to a lap pool. Movement, on the other hand, can be anything and can be anywhere. Movement is a motion that your body does with positivity and intentionality. Inside my gym, we have an area that I call a playground because that is basically what it is. You can get on there and move and strengthen and lift in whichever ways you prefer. It doesn't have to be one way or another. It can be your natural movement. If you are going to burn calories or pick something up and put it back down, it might as well be as enjoyable as possible.

I recently traveled to Mexico on a trip with a large group of fitness and health experts. We took a hike up to the top of Monkey Mountain, a popular spot due to the 360-degree view at the top. With this group, there was unspoken competitiveness that came across us all as we began to race up this mountain, everyone wanting to get to the top first. All of these fitness people are racing to the top. I used to be like that, but now I'm a little older, and maybe I've grown to see things a little differently. So, I intentionally held back and took my time enjoying the climb up to the top. I saw things that most others rushed past. One part of the hike brought us through these massive vines, and so I grabbed one and started to swing on it. It was a blast! I made it to the top, to the same place as everyone else, and I got to see the same view that they all saw. But by enjoying the journey, I got extra experiences and fun that so many others missed out on. It isn't about looking the best or finishing first. It is about getting the most out of life.

In my own fitness and health journey, I wanted to look good and feel better about myself. My pain gave me the motivation to be stronger and avoid being hurt again. As I've said, negativity is not a great motivator. I wanted to find some form of joy in what I was doing. Everyone talked about cardio, but I was not a huge fan of running. I had to open my mind to see outside of the box, the small box that I had put myself and fitness in. I started with a goal of 10 minutes a day for movement. This could be any form of activity that I want. Today, my current standard is a positive and intentional time of 45 minutes each day for movement. I can be out hiking, bike riding, or in the gym lifting weights, or I can be messing around on the playground. I am not limited to one particular routine or idea of what fitness looks like. I can explore new things and learn more about myself and how I move. As I began to discipline myself and commit to movement I could enjoy, I found that looking more fit and feeling better came along with that. My fuel and motivation are to move with positivity and intention, to love movement. This is necessary for purposeful exercise. Looking good is a bonus.

Movement is more significant than exercise because it is limitless. Movement is an intentional action that is not a part of your work or household chores. It is purely targeted towards your fitness, health, and enjoyment. What types of movement do you enjoy the most? How can you capitalize on those things and dedicate yourself to 10-45 minutes of movement each day? As I began to love movement, get stronger, and feel better—I found more and more exercises to be enjoyable. I actually run a lot more often than I used to. The line between movement and exercise is blurry in the best way possible as we find more and more joy in the building up of our bodies. Movement is fun. Movement is play. Movement is life. So, get out there and move!

SETTING THE STANDARD: LIMITLESS FITNESS

You will either set your standards by your life or live your life by your standards. When it comes to your fitness and health, what standards do you hold to? And what is driving those standards, you or the circumstances around you? Play offense with your life and with your standards. Most people know how to play defense: get more sleep when you feel sick, take a long walk after eating twice your bodyweight at a Thanksgiving feast, or drink some water in the morning after having a few beers the night before. We are good at responding to a health and fitness crisis because we are finally motivated to do more than the bare minimum. I challenge you to play offense. Pay the price for better fitness now by setting standards that proactively improve life and invest in your body's long-term health and wellness.

My goal is to help you move better, feel better, and live better—but I cannot make you create new habits or establish new disciplines in your life. You have to be in control of your presence in order to move and climb towards your future. Life will not make it easy for you to unleash your limitless fitness. You can't wait for your schedule to clear up or for your local gym to start sending trainers to your house to get you out of bed in the morning. Set the standard for your life and then live by it. I started with 10 minutes of movement each day, and I dedicated myself to growing that amount season by season. Every element has the opportunity for doubt: you can't run that far, lift that much, or dedicate that much time—those are all lies! If you can set standards for yourself and live by them, then you will be able to unlock and unleash your limitless potential.

1. Set the standard for your morning routine: you can control what time you get out of bed and start your day. There is an immense amount of research and science that supports the truth that your morning routine sets the tone for the rest of your day. There is not a magical time or hour to wake up. It is more about your positivity and intentionality. Hitting the snooze button sends signals to your body and mind that are

negative, and if you set the alarm on purpose, then hitting snooze derails whatever plans you had. Avoid setting your alarm with the intent of hitting snooze five times; I've heard people plan out their day by setting their alarm for 5:30 am because they know they need to get out of bed at 6:15 am, and they can't get out of bed without hitting snooze a dozen times first. Break that habit! That is planning to fail and starting your day with an "I can't get up the first time" story, which again makes a bigger impact on your body and mind than you realize. If you want to move better, feel better, and live better—then start by getting out of bed on purpose with purpose.

2. Set the standard of daily movement: be positive and intentional by dedicating time in your day to movements that you enjoy. Again, this doesn't include hustling down the hallway at work or standing at the grill in the backyard— this is an intentional movement that holds the sole purpose of growing your fitness and health. It also doesn't have to be a mundane workout routine or a carbon copy of some exercise that an influencer posted; it could be those things if you can find some joy in doing those movements. I'm just reminding you not to put fitness and health in too small of a box. Set this time and commit to it; do not let anything get in the way of you having this time. Use your best wisdom and discernment when selecting your time and the amount of time. I began with 10 minutes and grew to 45 minutes. I

also started with things that I loved the most: sports, dance, hiking, and weightlifting; from there, I learned and grew as I began to enjoy more and more different types of movement and exercise. From there, I made a commitment to get up and move during each hour of the day; 60 minutes never go by without me standing up and moving around. I also play with my kids each and every day, and so my entire day is now holistically rooted in movement. Build your life around movement. Repetitive daily motion is going to play the largest role in how we look, move, and perform. If you ever come to my gym, we will work with you to find your next best steps.

3. Set the standard of your daily diet: be positive and intentional with what you eat and drink. I hear people talk about feeling like garbage and not being able to move like they used to, and then I learn more about their eating habits. You cannot control what happens around you, but you can control what you eat and when you eat. There is plenty of research and science out there when it comes to diet, and there are even more opinions that you can find on social media or around the water cooler. I would guide you to take the same approach with your diet and your movement—do what comes most naturally to you that will help you grow and move forward in your fitness and health journey. Just because a friend found success with this type of diet doesn't mean you need to do it. Just because a celebrity endorses this type of juice cleanses or practices fasting does not mean it is best for

you. You will find better results when you find positive and intentional rhythms. Do not accept the limitation that eating healthy means eating bland or boring food. Do not believe the lie that making good dietary choices requires you to be wealthy. There is more amazing and affordable food out there for you to discover and enjoy. Set the standard and live by it, do not wait for a healthier menu to come find you.

4. Set your standard for finishing strong each day: when your day is coming to an end, you have your greatest opportunity to invest positive and intentional habits into your fitness and health journey. The truth is, the last hours awake each evening will set the tone for the following day. So much of how you move, how you feel, and how you live each day is established by what you did last night. If you want to find limitless potential in your health and fitness journey, then you need to set the right standards and habits for the end of every day. First, find time near the end of your day for meditation and reflection. Ask yourself how your day went and what you are thankful for today. Take some deep breaths and give yourself some positive affirmation. Ask yourself what tomorrow would need to look like for it to be a successful day. Second, schedule out tomorrow. Each night is when you decide when to wake up, prioritize what needs to get done, and schedule out all of the pieces. Life will never be perfect, and you cannot control everything, but you can tap into your God-given purpose and limitless potential by investing

positive and intentional planning into each day. The third and final piece to a strong finish is preparing everything you need for the next day; give yourself the tools to succeed for tomorrow. Some examples include: drinking water, avoiding late-night snacks and sugars, taking care of your body, and getting a good night's sleep. Everyone values sleep because everyone needs it. But for some strange reason, sleeping in and hitting the snooze button is considered cool and normal, while getting to bed by a reasonable time is considered lame and boring. Ignore that noise and set the standards that will give you the most fuel to succeed. Sleep is not a luxury; it is a necessity. Your body and mind need quality sleep, so give your body what it needs and unleash your potential each day by being positive and intentional each night.

5. Set the limitless mentality for your fitness and health: this mindset invites you to focus less on the finish line and look forward to each day along the way. The point of fitness and health is not to live forever; I'm sorry to tell you this, but one day you are going to die. Limitless fitness doesn't mean dunking a basketball, dropping down to your high school weight, or making the cover of a magazine. It simply invites you to grow and climb higher up the mountain each day. You need to believe that each day you can move a little better, feel a little better, and live a little better than the day before. When you focus on the journey and set standards for your

daily life, you will be amazed just how far you can go and how much your life can change for the better.

PAY FOR IT NOW OR PAY FOR IT LATER

I love this phrase; pay for it now or pay for it later. It inspires me, and it challenges me. Everything in life comes at a cost, which also means that everything in life comes with pain. You can either pay for it now or pay for it later. Here is what I mean by that. When we look at our fitness and health journey, we can all understand that our fitness commitments and standards will cost us energy, discipline, and focus. The five standards that we just went through all have a "pay for it now" cost involving daily habits and routines. Now, on the other side of this coin, we have the long-term effects of neglecting our fitness and health, the "pay for it later" option. This will ultimately cost us limited movement, limited feeling, and limited life. I can think of plenty of short-term examples like staying up way too late to watch three more episodes of a show; I will pay for that later when my alarm goes off, and I do not have the energy or clarity needed to start my day well. I have some gut issues from having my appendix removed; there are plenty of moments when I am choosing between eating what is right in front of me (and paying for it later) or making a quick choice to pass on that dessert (pay the cost now).

And then there are the long-term examples, which are so very real and so very important to understand. The daily choices we make now are impacting our future cardiovascular health, mental health, and muscular health. The longer the time frame we look at, the bigger the impact is. Whether positive or negative, our payment option creates a form of compounding interest in its impact on our body. This means that a long-term commitment to limitless fitness and health will make exponentially beneficial impacts on your life. The frightening reality for all of us is that a long-term lifestyle of paying for it later will accumulate with interest, creating a heavy toll on how we move, feel, and live later on. I can see the difference between people who make it a habit to pay for it now versus those who decide to always pay for it later; it is clear as day. Paying for it later will always lead to a limited life. And for many, a shorter life. I am in my early forties now, and people always think I am younger. They usually tell me that I must have great genetics or something, which really isn't true—I look young and healthy and fit because I've made the decision to invest in my fitness and health now and set the proper standards to live by.

No one is perfect, and we do not need to be perfect. You do not need to get it right all of the time, and you certainly do not need a perfect record in order to decide to do what is best for your fitness and health today. You can always turn the tide and begin to rediscover your purpose and limitless potential. The decisions you make today will impact tomorrow and further down the road. A friend of mine who is a pastor likes to say that our decisions ultimately lead us to a breakdown or a breakthrough. There isn't much in between. I believe that applies here to our fitness and health, and it certainly applies to the following chapters and discovering a truly limitless life. My hope and prayer for you are that you make the choice today to set your life up for a breakthrough. Unlock your limitless potential and find greater success in the area of fitness and health by investing in yourself today. If you are reading this, then you have breath in your lungs. Get out there and move with purpose! Be positive and intentional! Make the most out of the life that God has given you!

TAKEAWAYS & GROWTH QUESTIONS

In our first quadrant of success, I want you to understand that the way you move, feel, and life can grow each and every day. You have limitless potential! You are never too old or too broken down to move forward. Climb the mountain by taking the path that most inspires you to grow. Love who you are and love the potential that you have. You cannot control everything about your life or your body, but you can control your movement and lifestyle. Here are the key takeaways for this chapter:

1. Comparison is a thief of joy, but it is also a thief of potential. There are billions of people on this planet! This idea that fitness and health come in one shape and size is outrageous and harmful to the uniqueness of every person.
2. The way we believe, think, and talk about our fitness and health journey matters. One of the biggest weights and

obstacles that I find holding people back is the story that they are telling themselves.

3. Building positive and intentional moments in your day is like refreshing your heart, mind, and body with a cool glass of water. It can be hard to tell a better story when you are tired, depleted, and dry. Be positive and be intentional in your day-to-day life, and you will find more growth and joy in each season of life.

4. Life will not make it easy for you to unleash your limitless fitness; you can't wait for your schedule to clear up or for your local gym to start sending trainers to your house to get you out of bed in the morning. Set the standard for your life and then live by it.

5. You can either pay for it now or pay for it later. Unlock your limitless potential and find greater success in the area of fitness and health by investing in yourself today.

Take some time to go through these growth questions from this chapter on fitness and health. As always, you have several options for how you can work your way through them. Be honest with yourself and the people you may be sharing your thoughts with. The choice is always yours; choose to be authentic. If you have your own questions, then add them to your reflection and discussion! Here are the questions I'm offering for this chapter:

1. Where are you now in your fitness and health? Where do you want to go, and why?

2. On a scale of 1-10, how positive are you as a person? Also, on a scale of 1-10, how positive do you specifically feel about your fitness and health journey right now? What would it look like for you to be more positive?

3. What types of movement are you drawn to? What are some activities that you enjoy that get your heart pumping and get the sweat dripping?

4. What standards and disciplines do you currently have that support your fitness and health journey? What are the standards that you need to adopt into your daily life today in order to move better, feel better, and live better tomorrow?

5. Who is helping you and guiding you along your fitness journey? Where can you find accountability, encouragement, and coaching when you need it?

chapter ten

LIMITLESS FINANCES

"YOU HAVE THIS PRESENT MOMENT TODAY, BUT
TOMORROW IS NOT GUARANTEED TO ANY OF US.
TRUST ME, IT'S NEVER TOO LATE TO LIVE WELL AND
BELIEVE BIG ABOUT THE TIME YOU HAVE BEEN GIVEN.
TIME IS OUR MOST VALUABLE CURRENCY, AND OUR
SUCCESS WILL ULTIMATELY BE DETERMINED BY HOW
WE SPENT OUR MOST PRECIOUS RESOURCE."
JUSTEN ARNOLD

SAY IT AND BELIEVE IT

I refer to chapters nine, ten, eleven, and twelve as the four quadrants of success. These are the four main areas of life where our success and limitless potential shine brightest. This chapter is obviously focusing on the success and limitless potential of our personal finances. I know that some of this might sound cliché, but there is a life-changing truth about money and value that you need to say out loud to yourself and believe with all of your heart. Your success, value, and potential are not defined by how much money you have, what you accomplish, or what title you bear. Period.

"Yeah, yeah, yeah. Sure, Justen."

No, really, it is true. You are not a better person or more valuable person for having bigger assets, more followers, or a fatter wallet.

"Of course. I mean, that would be elitist and prideful."

That's true, and most people would agree with this premise. But, when societal pressures and expectations come crashing into our souls, we often act and live as if we don't. It's so easy to say but often so hard to believe.

In this chapter, I want to challenge each of us to say it and believe it. Most importantly, we need to live it out. Your success, value, and potential are not defined by how much money you have, what you accomplish, or what title you bear. Your purpose and potential are not rooted in the circumstances around you. They are found only in who you are, who you were intentionally created to be. As we unpack this truth throughout the chapter, you may feel some anxiety or pain from the expectations and pressures that you experience. Feel what you feel, process it, and move forward. There is greater success and fulfillment in life, limitless potential, and God-given purpose—hold on to what is good. You have so much life to live and joy to discover along the way. You are known and loved and valuable, no matter what. Say it and believe it.

THE STORY WE TELL OURSELVES: FINANCES & VALUE

We are consistently under the influence of the story that we tell ourselves. When it comes to finances and value, this is especially true. The way we think and talk about money, work, our home, our car, and our lifestyle all play a role in shaping our emotions and energy around these topics. We can tell a positive story with healthy definitions of success, finances, and value or tell a negative and harmful story. As always, the story we tell will manifest itself in various ways in our lives, for better or for worse. The story you tell about your life and your finances matters.

The greatest temptation we face is to think and talk about finances and value with a scarcity mindset. A scarcity mindset is deeply negative and destructive. This is the mindset that whispers to us, "you do not have enough" and "you are not enough." The scarcity of money, achievement and title comes from a place of emptiness, insecurity, and darkness. When our story is coming from scarcity, we are always coming up short and never feel content or happy with what we have. This type of thinking will make us forsake the good things all around us, and we will even devalue the people around us because we are too narrowly focused on having more of something else. Ultimately, the need to earn more and promote higher will isolate us from our other ambitions and priorities in life.

An unhealthy mindset on money can disrupt and devalue even the healthiest mindsets on other quadrants of success. Let's say someone loves their family, wants to provide for their spouse and kids because that fills them with a sense of purpose and value. With the wrong mindset, this person can begin to warp their self-image and self-worth as a provider in a way that leads them to believe that their only value and role is to provide money for their family. So, they work longer hours, put in extra time chasing a promotion, and exhaust themselves with work in hopes of bringing home even more money to provide for their family. While this is happening, they are neglecting their actual relationships with their family members and also neglecting their limitless fitness and health as well. The story they tell themselves is that by being busy, working harder and longer than everyone else, they are creating a better life for their spouse and kids.

I hate to say it, but sometimes I call this "The Disney World Complex." I've seen it before, and it is really sad. A family arrives at Disney World, and they are in line to get into the park. The young kids are excited, but they are tired from traveling to the park and getting up early that morning. The kids start to whine and argue amongst themselves, and suddenly the parent just goes nuclear on the kids. I've even heard a father tell his kids that he worked too hard and they paid too much money for them to whine and complain at Disney World. The kids are shocked by what is probably an uncharacteristic outburst, and then everyone just looks sad. It is a wild phenomenon, but you see it all throughout the day at these expensive theme parks. Bummer, right?

You see, Disney World is truly amazing, and I think you should take your kids there if you have the means to do so. However, the whole idea of "The Happiest Place On Earth" is kind of messed up. It is trying to sell you the mindset that it is ok to work the extra hours, neglect your family while you save up, then finally take them to the one place that will bring them overwhelming joy and happiness to make it all worth it. Then you get there, and your kids are just kids, and it's really hot and humid, and you drive forever to get there, and the illusion starts to crumble. Are kids difficult, and do we sometimes snap? Yes, but this is different. You can hear it in their voice and see it on their face. They had told themselves the wrong story, and it wasn't fulfilling them quite like they thought it would.

We tell ourselves this story that we are only worth what we earn, and we are as valuable as the money we provide. And so, we live each day focused on getting more so we can feel like more, and be more in the eyes of someone, maybe ourselves or maybe our family. This story is wholistically incomplete and incompatible with your purpose. Your value and worth are set in stone, and the story you tell about finances needs to reflect that. Your role in relationships with others is not defined by your job, income, or societal status. Your worth as it relates to your existence is not formed by the reputation or awards that you earn. Your success as it relates to your career is not measured by your money or your stuff.

We need to tell a better story. We all ought to feel confident and complete in who we are, regardless of what we have or what title we hold. The other mindset, the other story we can tell ourselves, is that who we are and what we have is enough. Another story to tell is that no matter what happens at work, what happens at the bank, or what happens in our house—we can have everything we need. There is nothing wrong with being ambitious, or getting promoted, or working hard. We should strive for all of that. We just need to avoid making that our identity and purpose in life. If our sole focus and identity is to be a millionaire, then we have two problems. First, we have limited our happiness and potential for financial success by making it conditional. Second, we have made the finish line our focus instead of the daily journey to get there. This means we will inevitably miss the value in the margins, the real daily moments of joy, and the potential that they each hold. Living with limitless finances means discovering the potential that is unconditional and enjoying the journey more than the destination. As I said in the last chapter, if we focus on living each day with purpose and potential, wealth will come, and it will be a blessing. Our true success and currency are greater than money.

TIME IS CURRENCY

If not money, titles, or assets—then what could our most genuine measure of success be? What story should be told in and through our life? If our success and value come from within, then what does that actually look like? How do we tell a better story?

I believe that our greatest and truest currency is time. There is a reason why we say that we are "spending time" when we are with someone else. Time is a precious commodity. No one knows exactly how much they have, but we all know that our amount of time is limited. We get to decide what and who we give our time to, what and who we spend it on. Everyone has 24 hours in a day, which also equals 1,440 minutes, or 86,4000 seconds. What do you spend your time on? Thinking about your time as currency changes the way you see the value of each moment. In today's culture, we are conditioned to view our education and work as the main priorities of our success and purpose. Then, once we are old enough, we can retire and purely enjoy what time we have left. Think about that for a moment. We spend roughly 20% of our time in school, then somewhere around 60% of our time working, only to enjoy the last 20% or less of our time in retirement. Ladies and gentlemen, not to be a downer, but more and more people are having to work longer and retire even older than they did before.

I don't know about you, but I do not like the proposition of waiting until my time is almost up to live my life to the fullest or act like my time is precious to me. I've said it before, and I'll say it again. Some people stop living when they start working, and they wait for decades until retirement to try and be human again. If you aren't living, then you are dying but not buried yet. You might be a zombie walking the halls at work every day waiting for permission to take a bite out of life. We are meant to live for so much more than this! All living beings are encoded with a desire to thrive and grow, to make their time count. When we exchange our time for money, we are selling ourselves short; we are getting ripped off. Stepping away from our purpose and potential leads to a breakdown, feelings of hopelessness, depression, and emptiness. This is no way to spend our time here.

Luckily, new bursts of life are available at all times. When we spend our time growing, thriving, discovering, and loving the world around us, then we are truly beginning to live! Time spent being creative, pushing through challenges, and finding new and deeper truths—this time is fulfilling and satisfying. When we spend time in life, we become enriched. True wealth comes from what we buy with the time we have been given. True success is found in spending our time, each day, in meaningful and purposeful ways. I believe that we were created and purposed to love, serve, and explore. So, I have to believe that my true currency of time should be spent doing just that. The more time I can spend loving my family, serving my community, and exploring the world around me—the richer and more successful my life becomes.

Some people believe that money buys them happiness or that money buys you more time. In a way, that is slightly true. Money is merely a tool that can afford you medical care and safety that may physically extend your time here on Earth. It is a tool that can buy you things that can be used to demonstrate love, provide acts of service, and facilitate your exploration of the world. BUT, and this is a big but, money cannot give your time purpose. At the end of the day, your time is your currency and how you spend it determines the success and wealth of your life. You do not have to wait until retirement to spend your time wisely or richly. You have this present moment today, but tomorrow is not guaranteed to any of us. Trust me, it's never too late to live well and believe big about the time you have been given. Time is our most valuable currency, and our success will ultimately be determined by how we spent our most precious resources.

I see influencers on social media challenging followers to grind and hustle for more money, to put in 80 hours in a week, and obsess about how much they can earn. Eighty hours in a week, they say it like it is a badge of honor. If you are in a season of life where your family truly depends on you to work that much, then I want you to know that I'm not talking about you. I hope that you find a way to change your position to work fewer hours, but trust me, I know that providing for our family is part of how we love them. I'm talking about the mentality that pushes people to make more money than they need, to sell their limited time on Earth chasing after a life of seven-figure incomes and Lamborghinis. Everything comes with a price because everything we do costs time.

When you are younger, it is easier to miss this point entirely. We believe we have so much time, so why not use it to chase the life of luxury that we think will bring us happiness? This thought process is broken and singular, a means to no end. All we have to do is look to the indigenous people of the world. What we will see is their level of joy and happiness and no signs of mental illness. They have closeness, they have community. They have true and lasting richness and luxury. There is research behind this. Even as we get older and start a family, we get trapped in "The Disney World Complex" and believe that the time we spend working late will all be worth it for one week-long trip to Orlando once a year. When we are making money, we justify coming home late, missing moments with our babies, missing ball games and recitals, and missing the margins in between that we didn't even realize were there. But what does that cost? Time. I'll tell you something that we all know, but I think we need this laid out in front of us. Think about the most amount of money that you've ever earned in an hour. Think about the most amount of money that you've ever earned in a day. I can keep going, but I'll stop here. Think about that amount of money. I do not know one person, nearing the end of their time here on Earth, who wouldn't spend that money just to go back in time for one single minute to hold their baby again; their best day's wages to have one minute back to see that view or stand on that beach or smell that fresh air. Money cannot buy more time; it cannot bring us back to relive the moments that we freely give away each day. This is a sobering reminder to live life to the fullest. Go to work tomorrow, but don't stay later than you have to. Work hard, but don't miss a moment that could truly enrich your life. The good news is we can make up for lost time, and we can start today. It just takes some positivity and intentionality.

LEAVING A LEGACY

Your time has the power to change the world. Each connection you make leaves an impact that ripples across time and space. When our wealth and value are defined by money, then we often fail to see the value in the people around us. If all we see in the mirror is a dollar sign, then that is all we will see in the people around us. History has proven that humanity has always struggled with the sin of judging based on social and economic class, among other things. We will continue to struggle with equality if we use money as the value and definition of ourselves and our neighbors. This cannot be our legacy. We must recognize the humanity in ourselves and the humanity of those around us.

Imagine for a moment that your life is like a giant cup filled with water. Your legacy is defined by how you pour out your life and your resources on those around you. Everywhere the water lands, a forest grows. When our cup is empty, those who come behind us will see the trees left behind when our time is up. The greatest legacy we can leave behind is the culmination of all of our life's wealth and success. Now, if you believe that money is the definition of our wealth and success, then you should start collecting for that pot of gold one day. No, we know better than that. Our legacy is the culmination of our time spent on Earth. What we leave behind are the memories and the moments we have shared with the world around us. Our legacy is so much less about what we earned. It is firmly established in where and how we spend our time.

This is how we become limitless with our finances, resources, and value. We invest ourselves in others. We plant gardens and trees in the lives of those around us. Our time is our greatest resource. We bless others with our time. When we realize loving and serving is a joy, then we can be even more generous with our time, resources, and finances. You will always be remembered more for what you gave away than what you earned. So, give freely! Give generously! Your time and resources are limited. You only have so much. But take your limited time and resources and invest it into your family, your friends, your neighbors—now your life, your finances, and value has been passed on and lives on in someone else. Who has impacted you the most by sharing their time, love, and service with you? Who has blessed you with resources and financial support? Who has added value to your life to make you feel richer and more fulfilled? You can be all of those things and more to those around you. In doing so, you honor those whose legacy you inherited, and you become part of something larger than yourself. This is the truest and most limitless definition of legacy.

SETTING THE STANDARD: LIMITLESS FINANCES

How do you currently feel about your financial situation? After reading through this chapter so far, do you feel comfortable balancing work and life? How are you spending your time, and who do you spend it on? I want to share a few notes and reflections that are meant to help you think through your standards and practices for your finances and resources. Remember, set your life around your standards, not your standards around your life. That means that you need to use your finances and resources to fulfill your purpose and unleash your potential, not find your purpose in potential through them. As you read through this section, begin to evaluate your current practices and principles and determine what adjustments you can make to grow and enrich your life.

1. Set the standard on how much your time is worth: each of us needs to establish what our time is really worth to us. The more we understand the value of our time, the better we can use it and share it. This standard will shape our schedule and priorities.

2. Set your standard for generosity: when it comes to sharing your time, talent, and treasures (it's great when everything starts with the same letter, isn't it?), you get to decide how generous you want to be. My advice is to be as generous as you can, stretch yourself each year, and find new ways to give and support others through the blessing in your life.

3. Set your standard for thankfulness: everyone can benefit from learning and practicing thankfulness in their life. Make intentional time to be thankful, meditate on the good things that you have, and celebrate your blessings. It will be a great way to tell a better story, and it will inspire your generosity.

4. Set your standard for your legacy: as you give generously, it is important to consider what to share and who to share it with as your legacy is formed through your life. Who will tell your story, and what will they say about you? What about your life will echo in the lives of others? This is when your finances and value become limitless when you take what you have been given and share it with the world around you.

5. Set your standard for restoration: this last one might be a surprise, but I want to remind you that rest and restoration are important parts of our life and are worthy of our time. We can get so focused on working, growing, giving, serving, exploring, but we need time to rest and refill our cups a little bit. We cannot control everything that happens in the world around us, but we can control and prioritize rhythms of rest.

NOTES FROM MY FINANCES & BUSINESS

It is easy to confuse the image that we present to the world with who we are. You are not your job title, your profile picture, or the car you drive. You are the accumulation of your time and the choices you make with it. I grew up near Naperville, IL, with two parents who worked and worked and worked. They held many titles and presented themselves to many different bosses and co-workers, and managers. All they ever were to me were Mom and Dad. As I experienced the pains of life, I knew that I wanted to be as present for my children as possible. There was a season when our finances were in shambles due to medical debt and job loss. I knew that a career change would help, so I began the journey of training, coaching, and operating my own gym. Now, fast forward, I've been operating my business in Rochester, NY, for many years.

If you are a newer coach, business leader, or business owner, then I'd like to share a few notes from my experience that may encourage and challenge you. You have likely seen some of the posts online from coaches who mentor other coaches and trainers. They often promise six-figure incomes and exponential growth for your business. I'd like to paint a slightly different picture. I remember when I reached the point when I was making around $5k each month, thinking that I was a failure and that all these professionals online were killing it compared to me. I found out that earning around $5k per month was close to the average, but I still wanted more. I was pushing myself to grow past $10k per month, to push my take-home salary into a six-figure territory and beyond. I was hustling and growing my business left and right with three kids at home.

Everything changed when I decided to set my business around my standards, and my standards were not focused on money. The top two standards for my business are to 1) value my time and 2) value my freedom. This meant that putting in the extra hours and for the extra money was not going to work any longer. We didn't actually need me to make hundreds of thousands of dollars; we were happy and content without it. It just felt like I was supposed to make as much money as possible. I hated money for a long time because I saw my parents spend a lot of time working and never being home. I also had my struggles with debt and food stamps in adulthood. Growing my business invited me to swing to the opposite end of the spectrum and spend my time and energy earning as much money as possible. But I was no longer on board with giving up that much time and freedom to earn something that I didn't need. So, I began to scale back my time at work. My new goal was now to lower my hours without lowering my monthly income. Over the last year and a half,

I've been able to get my hours down to 20 hours or less each week while maintaining the same level of income.

While this isn't as sexy as the hustle mentality that some people sell, I'm making more money per hour, and I am honoring my standards and making the most out of my time. Scaling back to 20 hours a week has allowed me to enjoy daily moments otherwise that I would have missed. This past year, I've spent more time with my kids and my wife than ever before. I have been able to attend sporting events and birthdays. I've been able to cook every meal for the family, write this book, and grow in my faith and personal development. If you told me years ago that I would be making this much money by working 20-25 hours per week, I would have laughed in your face. I love my job. I love what I get to do. And I love that I can use my job to positively influence the lives of so many people; I get to love and serve my clients and my community. I don't do this job for the money, which allows me to be better at my job, enjoy it more, and ultimately be more successful—all while living by my standards and spending more time with my family.

If you are in the training and gym space, I'll give you a few quick insights into how I lowered my hours and maintained my income.

1. I've been in this industry for a while now. I've used my time to develop a good reputation and become well-known in the community. This means I do not need much time to build an audience now because I have formed one over time.

2. I have an average client retention time of 9-10 months. Some are for years. This means that I keep my clients and do not need to spend much time searching for new clients each week.

3. I know my ideal client very well. I've mapped out my client journey from awareness to acquisition to retention and referrals. I have also honed in on clear messaging to attract and inform clients of my services.

4. I've accumulated a content library of hundreds of pieces of content that I can recycle and refurbish and syndicate as need be.

5. I set very clear boundaries and expectations on my time with clients, and I honor their and my boundaries so everyone is comfortable and feels like they can communicate well.

These notes represent a large part of my path to scale back my hours while maintaining a healthy and profitable business. If you are ever interested in learning more about my business or client ideologies, please reach out anytime.

TAKEAWAYS & GROWTH QUESTIONS

In our second quadrant of success, I want you to understand that finances and value are so much more than money. Much of this chapter is dedicated to pointing out what good finances are and identifying which pieces are not. But I also shared that our true currency and wealth is the time we have been given in this life. What you spend your time on is ultimately the definition of your wealth and success. Commit yourself to grow as a person and set your standards for limitless finances. Here are the key takeaways for this chapter:

1. Your success, value, and potential are not defined by how much money you have, what you accomplish, or what title you bear. Period.
2. When our story is coming from scarcity, we are always coming up short and never feel content or happy with what we have.
3. True wealth comes from what we buy with the time we have been given. True success is found in spending our time, each day, in meaningful and purposeful ways.
4. Our legacy is the culmination of our time spent on Earth. What we leave behind are the memories and the moments we have shared with the world around us. Our legacy is so much less about what we earned. It is firmly established in where and how we spend our time.

Take some time to go through these growth questions from this chapter on finances and wealth. As always, you have several options for how you can work your way through them. Be honest with yourself and the people you may be sharing your thoughts with. The choice is always yours; choose to be authentic. If you have your own questions, then add them to your reflection and discussion! Here are the questions I'm offering for this chapter:

1. Where are you now in your finances and wealth? Where do you want to be? Why?

2. What is your view on money and the role that it plays in your life? What value do you find in your money? How do your life's actions and priorities support what you say?

3. What is your response to the idea that time is your greatest and most precious resource? What is your time really worth? Where are you wasting the most time? Where do more of your time need to go?

4. What kind of legacy do you want to leave behind? Who made a big impact on you? How can you honor them by sharing what you received with someone else?

5. What standards of finances do you want to establish for your life? How can you practice gratitude and thankfulness for the blessing of your life? How can you be more generous with your time, talent, and treasure?

chapter eleven

LIMITLESS FAMILY

"LIFE ISN'T EASY ON YOUR OWN. I DO NOT BELIEVE
THAT ANYONE IS MEANT TO BE ALONE. AVOID
TELLING THE STORY THAT YOU ARE BETTER OFF
WITHOUT FAMILY, FRIENDS, OR COMMUNITY."
JUSTEN ARNOLD

BE ALL IN

Two of the greatest stories and movies of all time are both Christmas movies. You might be thinking I'm crazy. So many Christmas movies are childish and corny. Some are straight-up annoying. I may be one of the most positive and optimistic people you'll meet, but I am not the person who listens to Christmas music all year round. There is something about these two stories, these movies that genuinely speak to the human experience and the struggle we all face. Every so often, a movie captures our hearts and minds in a way that mirrors our feelings and hopes and our fears. Both of these movies explore the despair of isolation and joy of community and family. Each film invites us to be rooted in what matters the most, to be all in and fully invested in our friends, family, and community.

The first movie is called, *A Christmas Carol*. I'm betting that you are familiar with this one. Inspired by the words written by Charles Dickens, a handful of movie adaptations have been made and shared around the world. In my opinion, the *Mickey Christmas Carol* is the best, or at least I'm biased because my youngest daughter loves it. Anyway, the story is solely focused on one man who lived through deep pain as a boy and young man. As he grew older, his pain controlled him and compelled him to shut everyone out and build a financial empire to shield him from the world. It was easier to focus his life on money, but it was colder and darker and lonelier as well. The man's name was Ebenezer Scrooge, and he would be visited by three spirits who would come to save him from his impending terrible fate. Here is where things get really interesting. Scrooge didn't know that he was heading towards destruction. He didn't understand how poor and broken he was living alone with his fortune.

So, the first spirit represented Scrooge's past, and it showed him memories of a time when he was a wide-eyed and loving child. He once had family and friends. He once had a community that he belonged to. The spirit also showed him his moments of loss and pain, to which Scrooge pleaded to the spirit to stop and show him no more. The second spirit showed Scrooge the wonder and joy of the present, the adventure to be found in every moment, and the life and love to be found in every relationship. Living in the present is bright, and rich, and colorful. It invites us to be all in, fully present and soaking up everything and every connection. And then the third spirit came, showing Scrooge that he would suffer a terrible fate unless his life changed. His life would come to an end, and his legacy would merely be a grumpy old man who had nothing, despite his incredible wealth. The movie ends with Scrooge waking up on Christmas morning, ready to fully embrace his life in the present. The pain of his past and the fear of the future would no longer define him or limit him. He would live in the present and be all in. Scrooge became as good a friend, as good an employer, and as good a man as the city had ever seen. There is more joy when we are fully present in the present. That is truly our gift to ourselves and to the world around us.

The second Christmas movie that I'd like to touch on briefly is Frank Capra's *It's A Wonderful Life*. If you haven't seen this movie in a while, I challenge you to go watch it, even if it isn't Christmas time. This movie is inspired by a short story written by Phillip Van Doren Stern called "The Greatest Gift." In the movie adaptation, we see a very real-life play out in front of us. The story follows the life of a man named George Bailey. Here is the premise: George has always had big dreams and a big heart, but it feels like things just aren't going his way. He wants more for his life and wants more for his family and community. There is this rugged individualism. There is a belief that it is all up to us to fix everything and bring value to ourselves and our community. When things take a bad turn for George, he loses all hope and contemplates suicide. Life has always been hard for George, but he shoulders the pain and keeps going until he finally runs out of strength. If he alone cannot fix all of the problems, provide everything that he has ever dreamed of, or save the town that he lives in, then what is the point of his life? George wanted to care for his family, his home, his community, and his business—but he felt like a failure. Things never appeared to improve, and so he wondered if it all would be better without him.

I'll skip to the end because this really is a great movie, and you need to watch it again. George Bailey comes to understand that his life is wonderful, his life is rich. He receives a note saying, "remember, no man is a failure who has friends." His family, his home, and his community are far from perfect, but it doesn't have to be perfect to be the most precious and worthwhile adventure of his life. This man finds new hope and a new passion in his relationships and connections to the people around him. George had been shouldering it all on himself until he finally allowed his family and community to care for him. Perhaps my favorite thing about this movie is that while George realizes the beauty and richness of his life, in the end, most of his problems and struggles are still left unresolved. The town is still under threat, his home is still in disrepair, and his business is still an underdog. I believe this further proves the main point, that facing the struggles of life with loved ones by your side is the most wonderful life we could live. There will never be a day on Earth when everything is perfect. Something will always need to be done around the house, some friend or family member will need your help, and work will always have its ups and downs. But a wonderful life, a limitless life, is unconditional. We only need to be all in with the people around us because we are better and stronger together.

THE STORY WE TELL OURSELVES: FAMILY & COMMUNITY

When it comes to relationships, family, and community—what story are you telling through your life? How do you think and talk about your partner, your family, and your circle of friends? What do they all mean to you? Our words and thoughts matter. As we've discussed many times now, the story we tell ourselves plays a huge part in how we interact with the world around us; it impacts how we view and value our relationship with ourselves and our relationship with others. We certainly tell a story with our words and thoughts, but we also tell a story with our actions and priorities. The people around us will first hear our words and good intentions, but they will ultimately know us by our actions and the fruit of our efforts. Unfortunately, sometimes the story we tell limits the steps we take.

Our most precious resource is time, and we often say that our relationships are vitally important to our lives. Then we need to stop telling ourselves that we do not have time for our relationships! I found this to be the most difficult when I was first starting my business, and our family had grown with three children. I was often feeling worn out. There just wasn't enough time each day. I was helpless and bound by my responsibilities and the realities of adulthood; there wasn't any freedom to take control of my schedule. When it came to family, my focus was primarily on providing. When it came to the community, my focus was building my brand and client base. I just didn't have the time or energy to play, be around for meals, go on a date, or invest in friendships. That was the story I used to tell myself.

For the short season that I thought that way, I acted that way. I was wearing myself out, and I was wearing everyone else out when I came home tired and uninspired. Life is still full of pain and struggle. I still come home tired and worn out some days—but now I can recognize it faster and dig deep to adjust. Also, my family has healthy expectations of me. My friends have expectations. My clients have expectations. I decided to tell a better story: I do have time and energy for the people who matter the most. My community is not an untapped well of clients. It is a multicultural body of people who are worth knowing and serving. My family is my rock and my inspiration. I am going to give them my best and make quality time with them a standard for my life. After telling a better story for a season, it starts to become more and more of a reality and a habit to the point that the people around you know you by your actions and not just your words.

Life isn't easy on your own. I do not believe that anyone is meant to be alone. Avoid telling the story that you are better off without family, friends, or community. No one is stronger for putting the weight of the world on their back and trekking through life by themselves. The devil outside doing push-ups is hoping for you to stay isolated. He is salivating at the thought of knocking you down when you've got no support and no backup coming. Connections make us stronger; they strengthen our roots. Marriage is a lifelong commitment. Joining two people together, working through anything, and staying by each other's side. You know the devil is going to try and attack you there because a failing marriage will make you weaker. Your children are tied to your roots, they grew from you, and you give and receive strength from them. The devil outside doesn't want to see you be a good father or mother, he wants to see you isolated and alone. So, he whispers to us, "don't you have some more work to do? Aren't you too tired of this? Haven't you spent enough time at work? Your spouse and kids are just going to drain you"… and sometimes we believe him and repeat those same stories to ourselves.

The story you tell is important, with your words and your actions. Your family, friends, and community are a source of strength and support. Life is full of pain. Do not allow pain to conquer you by facing it alone. Do not repeat the cycle and cause your family and friends to experience pain because you refuse to work on yourself. Tell a better story. As I have processed my own pain from childhood, I knew that I wanted to give my family and friends more than what I got. Honestly, that is not meant to be an indictment on anyone. I believe we should all want that for our loved ones. But I do know that my parents had to work a lot, and I just wanted them to be home with me. I just wanted more than provision. I wanted protection and adventure. In the last chapter, I mentioned "The Disney World Complex," a sad story of a parent trying to buy an experience for their family. Disney is great, I love it and you should too. However, you can have an experience with your kids in the backyard, at a local park, maybe across the state, on a campground or hiking trail. There are moments to share and adventures to have each and every day! Don't spend your whole year gaining chips only to spend them all in one week on vacation.

A better story to tell is that family, friends, and our community is where our heart and soul lie. It is where we should spend what precious time we have, and our fitness and health will help us explore and enjoy every second of it. These four quadrants flow into each other. It is easier to tell a better story when we move better, feel better, and live better. It is easier to tell a better story with your relationships when you release money as the center of wealth and value. In this quadrant, the story you tell will ultimately be the impact and legacy you leave behind. Life is full of pain and obstacles; you have probably been through hell at some point in your life; don't give up on yourself or your family. The best and happiest days are ahead of you. So then get out there and give it all you got! Go all in! Give the people around you the best that you have to offer!

SETTING THE STANDARD: LIMITLESS FAMILY

I'm going to lean into parenting more than anything, but I want you to imagine your standards for yourself and your family even if you currently do not have any children in your home. Whatever your relationships look like today, you need to set standards for tomorrow and the next season of your life. We cannot control our family, friends, or community—but we can control how we engage and respond with them. It is our daily choices and priorities that will ultimately shape our relationships and influence those who are closest to us. Grand gestures are great. Big trips and vacations are amazing ways to make memories and celebrate relationships. But nothing makes a bigger or longer impact than the standards that we set for ourselves and our family. Be a strong leader for your family. Be more than a provider, be a protector. Protect your dreams and standards, and protect the hearts, minds, and dreams of your children.

1. Set the standard of being home: we obviously have roles and responsibilities out of the home, but we need to set a standard for the time when those roles and responsibilities end at the front door. Becoming a limitless family requires us to remove obstacles and limitations. Let work wait until tomorrow, put your phone away, leave your computer in the case. The standard of being home is the standard of being present, positive, and intentional with those in your home. There is always something or someone else trying to steal away your attention. Set the standard and live by it!

2. Set the standard of character and communication: no one can control the weather, what happened at work, or what happened on the ride home. But we can control ourselves

and set a standard for how we interact and respond to the people around us. This is not a call to be an emotionless or expressionless robot; it is normal to have a bad day or feel the pain that the devil outside just dished out. Setting a standard of character and communication means that no matter what happens outside of the walls of your home, you can communicate how you feel without lashing out or erupting at the people around you. Tell the truth, be fair, and share your emotions with your family. I know that I have come home after a long day and wanted to put on a good show for my kids, but I just end up getting frustrated because I haven't dealt with my pain yet. Let your family know, "Today has been a hard day. I would love to talk with you, but I need a minute to sit and breathe first. Would you like to sit with me?" The way you handle and respond to stress will set a tone for your family. Set the standard for the way you conduct yourself and lead by example.

3. Set the standard of what your children learn: school is great and local schools are doing their very best to teach and inspire the next generation. Some people say that the education system is "failing" the youth. It's not. Parents are failing them. School is meant to teach information, equations, writing, and language, but the home is where kids learn about life, purpose, and potential. Parents fail when they outsource life lessons to school, television, and social media. Kids are going to ask a lot of questions; it is in their nature. Where

do you want them to take their most sincere and curious questions about life? How can you make your home a safe place to learn and ask questions about purpose and value, and pain? If your kids watched and listened to you, what would they learn about life, fitness, finances, and healthy relationships? Set the standard for teaching your kids how to think and process the world around them.

4. Set the standard for adventure and memorable experiences: find daily time to do something fun and meaningful with your loved ones. Get outside and explore. Do something you love together. Then do something that they love together. Nature is a key element for me. I always take my wife and kids out on a hike or to a park. The possibilities are truly limitless. You can stay home and watch a movie or play a game. You can sit and talk for a little bit after dinner before everyone rushes off to their rooms. You can go for a drive or read a story together. Be creative! Have everyone in your family contribute ideas and put them on a wheel, and spin it to decide what fun activity to do together. No one has unlimited money or resources, but some of the best experiences in life are free. Build a rich life together full of adventure and memorable experiences.

5. Set the standard for forgiveness and restoration: there are a lot of great expectations and standards out there, but some get a little too carried away. It isn't fair or healthy to expect that life or your family is perfect. It isn't realistic or

practical to expect that everyone will get along all of the time. Normalize forgiveness and restoration among your family and friends. Forgiveness requires one party to acknowledge that they have wronged another member of the family, to say sorry, and ask for forgiveness. Now healing can take place, and the relationships can move forward. I have seen families sweep things under the rug, make excuses for each other, and do their best to hide the cracks in their foundation. Relationships grow more strained, and the roots that bind us together begin to wither. For most people, the hardest words to say are "I'm sorry," "You were right," and "Worcestershire sauce." Two of those need to be a regular part of our family discourse. Maintaining healthy relationships takes work, it takes honesty, and it takes commitment. Set the standard and establish a limitless home with relationships that last.

A PROMISE FROM ME TO YOU

You might be reading through this chapter and thinking that you've already got this covered. Great! I cannot encourage you enough to continue knocking this out of the park. It is making a bigger difference than you often see. The time I have spent with older clients has reinforced the idea from the last chapter: you either pay for it now or pay for it later. When it comes to family, the options are to pay the cost of time and standards now or pay the heavy price of regret and brokenness later. People tell me they wish they could go back and spend more time with their kids, spouse, and friends.

If you are reading this and thinking, I just don't have time each day for positive and intentional moments with my family or friends. Then I want to make you a promise. You have the time; you have everything you need. You may be afraid that one day you'll be that older person lamenting and regretting the time never spent on what mattered the most. That doesn't have to be your fate. You cannot control the world, but you can control your time. Change the perception of value, adjust the definition of success, use the most precious currency you have on the most precious gift you have been given. I know that life is complicated and busy; it isn't easy to sort it all out. But I promise you can figure it out. I promise that I am cheering you on. Remember, you are not in this alone.

There are coaches like me, pastors, counselors, and trusted friends that you could lean on to help. We can help identify what can be offloaded from your schedule and share tools to organize and prioritize your life around your standards. One tool I use is putting notes and quotes around in places where I know I will see them. For example, inside my truck, there is a note that says, "We only have 24 hours in a day." It reminds me not to waste time, and it honestly makes a difference when I need it. Another tool I use to help build out my calendar, I have a series of questions that I ask myself before adding a new thing to my schedule. What is my main intention with this project? Is this helping to accomplish my purpose? Is it a distraction? What does it cost in money and time? Could someone else be doing it?

There are many tools and resources for maximizing time and reducing waste in your schedule. Take action and make the investment today. Change your habits and set new standards. It is never too late to start leading and loving your family. I promise that you can do it, and it will make all the difference in the lives of those who are closest to you.

TAKEAWAYS & GROWTH QUESTIONS

In our third quadrant of success, I want you to understand that you are worthy of being loved and loving other people. Live your life by the standards that you set; do not become a slave to the circumstances around you. A limitless family will never be easy, and it will never be perfect. It only requires that we put in the work and make the right daily decisions to cultivate a healthy and happy home. You are better in community and relationships than you are alone. You are enough, and you have enough to be a hero to your kids. Here are the key takeaways for this chapter:

1. Be all in with the people around you because you are better and stronger together than you ever are alone.
2. A better story to tell is that family, friends, and our community is where our heart and soul lie. It is where we

should spend what precious time we have, and our fitness and health will help us explore and enjoy every second of it.

3. The standards you set for your relationship with your family are the foundation of the legacy that you will leave behind. The greatest gift you can give is your daily best for them.

4. Allow your family to be imperfect and complicated because it is. Help restore and reconcile relationships, lead by example.

5. Do what you love with the people you love. Play instead of clean if you have to. Just make it a priority to spend positive and intentional time with those closest to you.

Take some time to go through these growth questions from this chapter on *Family*. As always, you have several options for how you can work your way through them. Be honest with yourself and the people you may be sharing your thoughts with. The choice is always yours; choose to be authentic. If you have your own questions, then add them to your reflection and discussion! Here are the questions I'm offering for this chapter:

1. What was your example of family and community like growing up? What standards and characteristics did your home have, and how did it impact you growing up?

2. What are the pains and obstacles that try to steal your attention away from your relationships? How do you combat those and work through them?

3. Are there any standards for relationships and family that you already have in place? What standards do you need to add or strengthen?

4. Every family and every relationship has complications. What complications exist in your home, and how can you be positive and intentional in loving and serving through them?

5. What resources and support can you find to help encourage you in your pursuit of a limitless family? Who can provide encouragement, mentorship, and accountability?

chapter twelve

LIMITLESS FAITH

"HAVING FAITH THROUGH UNCERTAINTY IS A KEY
TO SUCCESS. THROUGH EACH DAY AND EVERY
OPPORTUNITY, I GET TO CHOOSE TO PLACE MY
FAITH IN MY PURPOSE AND POTENTIAL AND TRUST
THE GOD WHO KNOWS ME AND LOVES ME."
JUSTEN ARNOLD

I CAN ONLY IMAGINE

I turned 40 years old while writing this book! Pretty amazing
to look back at my life and view the road that brought me here. It
is amazing to think about how much my life has changed over the
past twenty years. Well, now you know a lot of that story and how
much things have changed, don't you? Who would have guessed
that I would have an amazing wife and three children, that I would
be a fitness and health coach and own a gym, or that I would work

25 hours a week and earn all the money that I need? Today I move better, feel better, and live better than I ever have. It makes me wonder how I will move, feel, and live twenty years from now. If standards are kept, if the payment is made now instead of later, and if time is spent on the right people and priorities, I can only imagine what the future will hold.

Writing this book has been a wild adventure, and I am so honored that you have come this far to hear my story. To be honest with you, I've sat and cried a few times, thinking and writing about my childhood. The pain, the loneliness, and the desire to be seen. The pain is real. But so is the purpose. There was a seed of childlike faith that helped push me forward through my elementary and middle school years. Children have a curiosity and imagination that adults often let slip away as they grow older. When I look back at those dark times now, I cannot quite explain what kept me going. I can only imagine that each soul is given a God-given spark, an internal and eternal light. No matter how dark life gets, there is always that light to guide children forward.

As we grow and develop into adolescence and adulthood, that spark will either grow brighter or start to wane. It is clearly in my nature to be bright, optimistic, and energetic. However, the physical and emotional pains that I had suffered were leading me down the darkest of paths. I began to believe that my existence was only fit to be snuffed out like a candle in the wind. I held on a little longer. The hope of going off to college was inspiring and fueled my spirit. I knew that something had to change. I felt the pressure like it was all on me to make my life worth something, to make my purpose and pain make sense, and create a life for myself out of nothing. No pressure, right? I'm 18 years old, and it is all on me to figure out my future. I can only imagine how much I would have struggled. I can only imagine what could have happened if I hadn't heard the good news if I hadn't found my roots.

THE STORY WE TELL OURSELVES: FAITH IN OURSELVES, FAITH IN SOMETHING HIGHER

Well, this is the last chapter, so it's the last time I'll say that the story that you tell yourself matters. Welcome to limitless faith, a chapter about believing in yourself and believing in something higher. I don't know where you are in your faith journey, but I want to challenge you to remain open to what I have to share. You've stuck with me this long, hold on a bit longer and let's see if there is a spark in here for you. No matter where you fall on the spectrum of faith, I want you to believe that your faith can grow. That may mean planting the first seed and watching it sprout. It may mean building and nurturing your daily habits. It may mean reconnecting to the childlike faith in yourself and the world around you that you once had.

An honest question: how can we have faith in ourselves and something higher when there is pain all around us? It is a tough one, but let's zoom out a little bit and jump back into my story for a minute because I wrestled with this early on as my faith first began to grow. If you remember, it was the summer after I graduated high school when I encountered good news at a retreat with some friends. My friends Justin and John invited me to a faith-based conference over the weekend. I remember thinking that I was headed off to join some kind of cult, but I loved my friends and trusted them enough to tag along. When I got there, I was blown away! The community was amazing. The love and connection between people was something I hadn't seen before. There were large presentations from the main stage, smaller breakout classes, and places to ask big and difficult questions. The conference had the word "awestruck" in the name, and that is exactly how I felt.

I was immediately attracted to a breakout about dinosaurs—they are cool, and that was a topic I didn't expect to see. Then I was interested in what was being shared from the main stage. It was good news! There is something, someone higher than I am, and He sees me and knows me. No matter what has happened to me, no matter what I have done, He has a positive and intentional plan for me. This God is so generous and good that He took on the form of man and bridged the gap between Heaven and Earth by coming to be with us. He came for a reason, to freely give His life so that all of the world may know that they are loved and worth dying for. It wasn't just any death. Jesus gave His life on a cross—an agonizing and unbearably painful death. Yet, he used His voice to call us to life and love, even as He hung dying on the cross. Anyone who calls on the name of Jesus is saved from the brokenness of this world and the brokenness inside of them. Everyone is invited to be adopted into the family of God, and apparently, "everyone" includes me.

I had to process this quickly. I knew pain. I knew trauma; so, what was this? It was a moment to choose which story I would tell. First for myself: am I worth knowing, loving, and dying for? Is there more to my life than what has happened to me or what I've done? Can the parts of me that are broken be healed and grow? The spark inside exploded into a ball of fire. I believe that the answer to all of those questions is "yes." Now, do I believe that there is a God? Do I believe that He sees me and knows my pain? Could He have a positive and intentional plan for my life? There is a spark in all of us, and on that weekend, my spark burned bright. Where did our spark come from, if not from a God who created us on purpose and with purpose? With all of the pain, there are rays of light in family and creation and movement. Where does this light come from, if not from God? Our existence is not an accident. If it was, then nothing would have a purpose. In a way, the pain wouldn't exist without a purpose. Cold only exists as the absence of heat, and darkness only exists as the absence of light. Pain only exists in the moments that creation moves in contrast to God's positive and intentional purpose.

I didn't have all of the answers (I still don't, and I am not planning on it), but I had a budding faith that all of these things were true. I have a God-given purpose. God knows me, and Jesus died for me. I am a son of God, and I have everything that I need. Through the years, I have made mistakes, wrestled with doubts, and asked more questions. The spark continues to grow, and I continue to have faith in myself and faith in God. I believe that I can move better, feel better, and live better. I have faith that I can use my time and resources to make an impact on the world. I believe I can love and serve my family and community each and every day. And I believe that my faith will only grow stronger. God never promised a pain-free life, but He has promised us His love and presence to see us through whatever comes our way. In the end, we will all come to the end of our time here on Earth. When that time comes, I have faith that God will deliver us to an eternal life with Him in Heaven. There will be no more pain, only life, and existence in fullness.

This is my faith journey. This is the story that I tell and the story that I try to live out each day. Never perfect, but I still am trying to do my best to tell it and live it well. What do you believe about yourself? How do you describe what you believe about your purpose and potential? What do you believe about God? How do you describe what you believe about the good news and the Gospel of Jesus? My intention and hope is that you take one step of faith in each season of your life. What would it look like for your faith to grow? What could be your next step on your faith journey?

THE HAVES & HAVE NOTS

Our pain from the past and our fear of the future are constant struggles. As a society, we tend to use past performance and results as a way to measure present value and future potential. We also like to hedge our bets on the future by leaning into what feels most familiar or safe. The more complicated the past, the more unknown and unpredictable the future, the more we want to stay clear of that person or opportunity. When using these criteria to judge who has "it" and who doesn't, the haves and have nots are more than phrases. It is a system by which our world operates. One awesome example of this that we see every year is in the NFL Draft. This is when the professional teams gather together and select the players that they believe have what they are looking for.

They weigh their past performance and project the current value and future success. Some players have high production but also have off-the-field concerns or injury history. Their physical traits are also tested and measured; all of the data are pulled together in an attempt to make decisions with certainty. Sounds pretty good, right? The only problem is, this is a subpar way of evaluating purpose and potential. Each and every year, there are numerous players who fall short or grow beyond their projections. My favorite example is the draft of 2000. America had just survived Y2K, and it was time for another round of new talent to enter the National Football League. The opening rounds got started, and players were flying off the draft board.

When the 6th round came, teams were beginning to wind down their search for stars and were truly now on the hunt for role players and backups. With the 199th pick in the draft, the New England Patriots selected Tom Brady, a quarterback from Michigan. That is correct; 198 players, 6 of whom were quarterbacks, were selected before him. As a guy from Rochester, I can tell you that there are not a lot of Tom Brady fans around this part of the country. Between Tom moving to Florida and Josh Allen becoming a dominant player for the Bills, things are looking up for our football community. But for the point of this story, we will give this guy some credit. At the time of writing this book, Tom Brady has been to ten Super Bowls and has won seven of them! No one else from the 2000 draft class is still actively playing in the NFL, and neither is anyone from 2001, 2002, or 2003 draft classes. The man who might be the greatest quarterback of all time was the 7th quarterback picked in his draft; I still can't get over that! The point is past performance and experience is not always an accurate measure for present value or future potential.

We may wrestle with belief today because of pain or failure from our past. God is inviting us to have faith in ourselves and have faith in the opportunities before us, but we are too caught up in the past to believe in ourselves. On the other hand, we can become too stressed over the unknowns of the future. What will happen next if I say "yes" and have faith in myself or something greater than myself? Fear of the future is a real obstacle to faith and confidence in the present. The truth is, no matter what the past was like, and no matter how clear the future looks, we all have to decide whether or not we will have faith today in the present. Nothing is more important than the daily choices that we make. Starting a family, launching a new business, setting new standards to live by—I did not have any guarantees for my future based on my past. Having faith through uncertainty is a key to success. Through each day and every opportunity, I get to choose to place my faith in my purpose and potential and trust the God who knows me and loves me.

CHILDLIKE FAITH

I can repeat part of our conversation on being childlike and not childish. When it comes to faith, there is a huge difference between the two. Children have that God-given spark inside them, a genuine belief in seeing things that no one else sees. One of the many amazing stories in the Bible is about a time when Jesus fed thousands of people. He had drawn a large crowd in a remote location when it came to the attention of Jesus and his disciples that everyone was hungry. I mean, we are talking about a remote location, thousands of people, no food. The practical adult side of me wants to tell everyone, "well, that is what you get for not packing a lunch." Instead, the disciples, the men who followed and studied under Jesus, tried to sort it all out with real-life solutions involving money and resources. It seemed as if nothing could be done for this crowd of hungry people, and the disciples were about to tell everyone to go home when a kid suddenly stepped up to help.

The only problem was that this kid had a couple of fish and a couple of loaves of bread on him. The disciples were about to turn him away, which makes sense to us because how could that amount of food make any impact on a crowd this size? Imagine bringing a twenty-piece chicken nugget tray to a sold-out concert and offering to share it with the entire venue. But let's take a look at what is really going on here. I don't think we should really believe that the kid actually believed that the amount of food he offered was going to feed everyone. I believe that he simply wanted to help, so he went all in, gave everything he had in hopes that something big might happen. It is safe to assume that this kid was not the only person present who had food on them. However, he is the one and the only person who brought what little he had and laid it all out for Jesus to use. That is childlike faith. Jesus took the boy's food, gave thanks, and miraculously shared it with thousands of people that day.

People scoffed at the kid when he brought his food to share with Jesus. The practical and experienced adults could not imagine that anything other than the full amount would help because they were too narrow in their thinking, and their faith was too old. The boy with childlike faith believed that giving his all would make a difference, and it did! He had faith that somehow, someway, trusting in God would lead to something great. You and I are invited to live with childlike faith. We do not need to have the full and final product complete; we just need to take what little bit and believe that something greater can come. Adults can put off a dream, avoid a challenge, and ignore their purpose and potential because they haven't figured it all out yet. A person with childlike faith has greater trust in their dreams and in the adventurous opportunity that God is calling them to. They want to be a part of something bigger and better. We should desire that too.

SETTING THE STANDARD: LIMITLESS FAITH

All of these quadrants are deeply personal, including this final focus on faith. I want to share my insights and experiences through the standards that I have set for myself. Like everything else, our faith journey is like climbing an endless mountain. We are not going to reach the top. We aren't going to be perfect. We won't have all of the answers. That is ok. Give yourself some grace while also holding a healthy amount of humility. We get to enjoy the journey, learning and growing as we move forward. Limitless faith is found in the peace, love, and joy that we hold no matter what comes next. Always be growing, loving, and serving. These standards can apply to your life in whichever way you choose to utilize them. Be positive and intentional with your journey, and faith doesn't grow accidentally.

1. Set the standard for self-affirmation: the story you tell yourself is a powerful tool, don't waste it! I have mentioned already that I use meditation and mantras to help affirm and inspire myself throughout the day. My go-to routine is taking six deep breaths, and saying "I am a son of God. I have everything that I need." The physical action promotes relaxation and clarity, and the mental and spiritual action draws me to my roots and gives me strength. I have notes and quotes and Bible verses spread all throughout my home, car, and gym. Set the standard of daily affirmation by establishing time and rhythms of hope and inspiration in your life.

2. Set the standard for faith community: we are all the better in a community than we are on our own. When it comes to building a faith community, we can focus on our two main avenues of faith. First, we need to build a community around the faith we have in ourselves. We need to find a collective of people who inspire us, challenge us, and speak truth into our lives. The ideal community would be a well-rounded group of friends, mentors, coaches, and family. These are the people who will believe in you and help you believe in yourself. When the devil is outside doing push-ups, these people are ready to stand by your side and fight with you. Second is the community that supports and inspires our faith in God. God has a plan and design for a faith-filled community through the local church. Finding and connecting with a body of other believers is vitally important to our faith. We are stronger and healthier together. Set the standard of building limitless faith through the community.

3. Set the standard of seeking more understanding: we will never know it all, but we ought to continue learning and growing through each season of life. Seek to understand more about yourself by exploring tools and resources like counseling, personality profiles, and picking up new skills and hobbies. Seek to understand more about God and His purpose for your life by investing in quiet time, reading, studying, prayer, and exploring creation. There is limitless potential when it comes to learning and growing in faith.

Make it a standard to constantly be stretching yourself and strengthening your faith through daily disciplines.

WORTHY

Life is a journey of highs and lows, wins and losses, mountain tops and deep valleys. We must navigate these well if we're going to live a productive and fulfilling life. No one has earned more worth or lost their worth based on their life. The price of our life was firmly established when Jesus decided to give everything up for us. There is a God-given purpose and limitless potential inside of you. We must willfully and joyfully grab hold of it. Everything we need is there. We just need it in a manner that is worthy of the purpose and potential that God has placed in us. It is like the sword in the stone or Thor's hammer—we do not create or add power. We, instead, must live in a way that accesses and unleashes the power inside. No person is worth more or worth less than anyone else; it all comes down to who is willing to pull the most out of themselves and live their life to the fullest.

I struggle with feeling worthy. My past and my pain are reminders of my brokenness. The devil tries to throw those things in my face and scream at me, "you are not worthy!" It takes faithful reminders to know that my worth comes from God, and no matter how many times I fail, I can live in my purpose and unleash my limitless potential each day. My hope and prayer are that you do not take your God-given worth, purpose, or potential for granted. Let your light shine bright, and let each step of your journey be a new discovery of how rich life really is. Pain hurts. Purpose and potential are stronger. You are stronger. Live in the strength that God has given you. It is more than worth it.

TAKEAWAYS & GROWTH QUESTIONS

Welcome to the end of this book. It has been an honor to share my story and my heart with you. A lot has been covered through these chapters. I hope that you have been encouraged and challenged to live life to the fullest. In this fourth and final quadrant, we discussed limitless faith. Limitless faith is the belief in yourself and belief in God to get you through anything. Take comfort in knowing that your life matters—your faith matters. Hold tight to the faith that you have in yourself and the faith you have in God. You have God-given purpose and limitless potential. Never let anyone or anything take that belief away from you. Here are the key takeaways for this chapter:

1. We all have a spark of faith inside of us. The daily decisions we make either inspire that spark to grow or diminish. In every season of life, our faith in ourselves and in something bigger than ourselves should grow.
2. Having faith through uncertainty is a key to success. Past performance and future fears will try to rob us of a present joy.

3. You and I are invited to live with childlike faith. We do not need to have the full and final product complete; we just need to take what little bit and believe that something greater can come.

Take some time to go through these growth questions from this chapter on faith. As always, you have several options for how you can work your way through them. Be honest with yourself and the people you may be sharing your thoughts with. The choice is always yours; choose to be authentic. If you have your own questions, then add them to your reflection and discussion! Here are the questions I'm offering for this chapter:

1. How would you describe the faith that you have in yourself? What has influenced those thoughts and feelings the most?
2. How would you describe the faith that you have in God? How did you arrive at those beliefs, and who helped shape them the most?
3. What would it look like for you to grow your faith in this season? What standards of faith do you currently hold? What standards of faith are you going to add?
4. What is an area of your life that you have the most faith in yourself? Why? And what areas of your life do you need to believe in yourself more?
5. Who is, or who could be, part of your faith community?

6. What are your greatest obstacles of faith in this season of your life? How can you grow past them?

final thoughts

While writing this book, Covid-19 interrupted life as we knew it. We had to stay home, wear masks, and social distance. Fear was in the air. We were scared. We were angry. We lost jobs, lost loved ones, and with no end in sight. We all made sacrifices. Some found purpose. Some lost it. We all had to pivot to navigate with the disruption. But, if you're still here after reading this book, life has proved you can endure. You have potential and a higher purpose.

Then there was the death of George Floyd. Tension was high with protests, looting, riots, and outrage. At times, I was even worried about my gym downtown being affected by all this. As a biracial family and a wife in the media, we suffered racist and discriminatory attacks. But still, I wrote. And many of you are still here with even more drive and purpose fighting for equality and justice, all sparked from some drama-filled severe pain.

During these tumultuous times, we started to prioritize what matters and find purpose. We got to know our families more by having deeper conversations digitally. We had to slow down and be still and enjoy each other more because *we didn't know* what the future held. So we prayed, loved, cried, marched, screamed, and wrote. I saw more people lifting up others and helping.

Like I talk about in this book, while you are alive, the devil, drama, pain, trauma, call it what you will, will come after you in the weirdest, wildest, and most unexpected times. But, I hope that you will have the power, strength, and mental fortitude to find purpose and meaning through it all and live the most fulfilling and impactful life possible. And if you need references, reminders, or motivation, you can always look back and find it in this book.

more from Justen Arnold

If you would like to connect with the author, Justen Arnold, and learn more about his training, coaching, and business, then please find and follow Justen on social media.

You can visit his website for more tools and tips on unleashing your limitless potential in fitness, finances, family, and faith.

JustenArnold.com

Want to check out Justen's gym and fitness career? Then check out the FlexxMP website! Or, if you are ever in the Rochester, NY area, come by and visit Justen at his gym.

FlexxMP.com

Start your day off with gratitude, record your wins, and keep track of your fitness and nutrition. We all need tools to help us conquer each day and build better habits. You can use this link to download and use Justen's daily journal, a tool crafted to help you change your life for the better. You can use it on your phone/tablet/computer or print it out. After downloading, you will receive a video from Justen that will walk you through some best practices for journaling. Justen looks forward to sharing this with you and would love to hear how you use it to crush your daily routines and grow in every season of life!

FlexxMP.phonesites.com/flexxmpjournal

acknowledgments

Not only so, but we also glory in our sufferings, because we know that suffering produces perseverance; perseverance, character; and character, hope. And hope does not put us to shame because God's love has been poured out into our hearts through the Holy Spirit, who has been given to us.
Romans 5:3-5 (NIV)

As I talked about at the beginning of this book, it took a team to accomplish this project, which I thought was just a dream. Certain people helped with this more than I could have imagined in ways you wouldn't normally fathom when writing and publishing a book. I can't name everyone, but if you've been referenced in this book or connected with me in some capacity on this project, you played a tremendous part, and I thank you.

First and foremost, I want to thank my wife, Alexis. You are my chief LIFE editor, my truest companion, and one of the main reasons I am the man I am today. Thank you for your love, fortitude, unwavering support, strength, and compassion for a man like me. Thank you for never judging me for my past or present and only loving me more each day. So many times, you could see and believe in things at times I could not. I don't know how I became so blessed to call you wife, but I thank God every day for you. (Just read my journal.)

Thank you, my children: Aaralynn, Jaelyn, and Ayva. Your all's energy, encouragement, and things I learn from you refuel me every day. You help me chill, give me the opportunity to be a kid again, and remind me everything is alright. I'm grateful for your support, patience, and love while writing this book, along with the opportunity to be your father. Being DAD to you all is the greatest, most fulfilling, and rewarding job I'll ever have. I feel blessed to see how some of the lessons I talk about here play out in real life with you all. I only hope and pray you all are better humans than I in this life. And in so many ways, all three of you already are.

To my brother Sean, thank you for your constructive feedback, tough love, honesty, and support when I needed it most. Not sure where'd I'd be if you weren't born my older brother and played the role you've played in positively impacting my life and this book. I love you, man.

A huge thank you to my good friend Justin H for the vision. Thank you for inviting me on a mission trip to the Dominican Republic in 2020. Thank you for long deep conversations about everything and then your strong encouragement to write a book. I remember it as if it was yesterday. "You should write a book! You have to tell your story!" Those words were the spark that began even the thought process of turning maybe into "I HAVE TO!"

Thank you to my Publishing Company, Two Penny Publishing. Thanks for believing in this project, along with the amazing team of people who helped make this book a reality. Specifically, Tom G. for saying YES to *Purpose Through Pain* and our long conversations filled with ideas, direction, and even book cover ideas. Thank you, Jodi C., for so much along the way, from communication to decision making, to editing to cover, and more. You are an incredible professional and human I'm grateful to know. Matt G., you were with me every step of the way and someone I didn't know before Covid-19, who I now can call a good friend. I also want to thank Kaylee S. What a joy it is to work with you and your marketing genius. Plus, we will always have a laugh from our first awkward meeting. I'm laughing now, thinking about it. Of course, there's more, but I want to thank Sarah W. and Jennifer M. during this process as well. You both played huge roles in getting this to publishing, and this wouldn't be the book without you all.

I also want to thank Tim D. and Mike L. While it might not seem like much, your all's helpful advice and guidance along the way, including our Saturday meetings, had great and positive effects on not only this book but on my life during the process of writing it.

Thank you to Kathryn Coakley Carangelo for taking the thought provoking and intimate time to take amazing photos of me in my element and capture beautiful moments with my family. It truly was a pleasure.

Thank you to the many friends, my pastor, and my church. You prayed for me and supported this book from the beginning.

And this might sound unconventional and give you an eye twitch, but I want to thank those who may be responsible for past pain and trauma. I am thankful for the painful, uncontrollable moments, the accidents, the hurt, the heartache, and the neglect. There were lessons to be learned in these moments, things to grow from and witness, and without them, I would not be the man, the father, the husband, the entrepreneur, and the author of this book. I would not have stories and moments to share that are helping people RIGHT NOW, and not just with this book!

I also want to thank you, the reader. I appreciate your support in purchasing this book, and thank you for your time in reading it. As I've mentioned, the most valuable resource is called TIME! So THANK YOU! I hope this book helps you and others as it has helped me in the therapeutic processes of writing it.

And finally all of this! My positive life, this book, everything would not be if it weren't for my Creator. I am thankful for God's guidance, Jesus' teachings, His belief, and His trust in me, especially in some of the hardest moments of my life. Because of Him, I've not only survived but thrived. I wasn't always a believer, and I felt lost and broken. This complicated puzzle called life started to piece itself together one at a time once I found faith. The puzzle is nowhere near being finished, but with God, I know it's going to be bigger and better than it could've been without him. If you're not a believer in something bigger than yourself, I highly encourage you to explore and learn all you can about as much as you can before you make a "final" decision. It could change your life and your afterlife.

God Bless

about the author

Justen Arnold is a committed husband, active father of three, adventurer, nutritionist, strength and conditioning coach, musician, best-selling author, public speaker, consultant, and multi-certified Movement & Life Optimization Coach.

Justen is from the Midwest and currently resides in Western NY. He has lived everywhere from Kentucky to Illinois to Iowa.

He is the Founder of Flexx Mobility & Performance, a multi-faceted health, and wellness organization, and host of the successful podcast One Step Further.

With more than 15 years in the health and fitness industry, Justen also runs a popular YouTube channel. In addition, he has written or contributed to dozens of articles for various blogs, publications, and podcasts.

As a survivor of severe childhood sexual and psychological abuse, attempted murder, and severe trauma, Justen is on a

 mission to take care of all people, whether it's families, individuals, or acquaintances, through his holistic philosophy regarding physical, nutritional, mental, and spiritual well-being.

He believes if people have access to the best tools and knowledge in a sympathetic environment, they will achieve their fullest human potential. This book is one of those tools.

When he's not working out, reading, or writing, you can find him hiking, playing drums, drawing, or meditating. Justen believes to be the best version of yourself, you have to do the inner work and find time to love and work on yourself. He hopes this book helps you in that journey.

Justen also regularly donates to and volunteers with various organizations, including his church and mission work with GO Ministries.

Made in United States
Orlando, FL
04 February 2022

14408409R00133